INTEGRATED
TACTICAL
PLANNING

INTEGRATED
TACTICAL
PLANNING

Respond to Change,
Increase Competitiveness,
and Reduce Costs

ROD HOZACK | TODD FERGUSON |
STUART HARMAN | AND DAWN HOWARTH

WILEY

Published by John Wiley & Sons, Inc., Hoboken, New Jersey.
Published simultaneously in Canada.

For general information on our other products and services or for technical support, please contact our Customer Care Department within the United States at (800) 762-2974, outside the United States at (317) 572-3993 or fax (317) 572-4002.

Wiley publishes in a variety of print and electronic formats and by print-on-demand. Some material included with standard print versions of this book may not be included in e-books or in print-on-demand. If this book refers to media such as a CD or DVD that is not included in the version you purchased, you may download this material at http://booksupport.wiley.com. For more information about Wiley products, visit www.wiley.com.

Library of Congress Cataloging-in-Publication Data

Names: Hozack, Rod, author. | Harman, Stuart, author. | Ferguson, Todd, author. | Howarth, Dawn, author.
Title: Integrated tactical planning : respond to change, increase competitiveness, and reduce costs / Rod Hozack, Stuart Harman, Todd Ferguson, Dawn Howarth.
Description: Hoboken, New Jersey : Wiley, [2021] | Includes index.
Identifiers: LCCN 2020046413 (print) | LCCN 2020046414 (ebook) | ISBN 9781119784753 (hardback) | ISBN 9781119784777 (adobe pdf) | ISBN 9781119784760 (epub)
Subjects: LCSH: Business planning.
Classification: LCC HD30.28 .H699 2021 (print) | LCC HD30.28 (ebook) | DDC 658.4/012–dc23
LC record available at https://lccn.loc.gov/2020046413
LC ebook record available at https://lccn.loc.gov/2020046414

COVER DESIGN: PAUL MCCARTHY
COVER ART: © GETTY IMAGES | HIROSHI WATANABE

SKY10023883_011221

Contents

Preface

Unlocking the Greatest Management Secret

We have long believed that Integrated Tactical Planning is the 21st century's greatest management secret in that best of companies simply "execute" all the time without stopping to think about whether they are doing the right thing at the right time. Our experience and observations suggest there is scant evidence of consistent methods and standard terminology to define best practices and that many companies do not know what these practices look like. In writing this book, we have been able to release some of the great practices we have deployed when we were in the industry ourselves and, more recently, some of the stunning successes we have had engaging with our clients. One of the standout findings through our research is that every Oliver Wight consultant would insist that there is a weekly replanning process deployed to support a company's monthly management process. Full stop. This may sound simple and reasonable, but where is the background literature to support how this is best achieved? Even when speaking with our software alliance partners, there is some functionality designed within the application, but it is non-standard terminology and typically a silo functional view at best. We intend to make Integrated Tactical Planning an industry standard term and elevate its understanding from ad hoc to defining something that all companies can, and indeed, should be doing. Most important, we would like to share the benefits realized by clients who have embarked on the Integrated Tactical Planning journey to offer a perspective on how it might help your organization and improve the lives of customers whom you ultimately serve.

Who is this book for? This is intended as an executive synopsis of Integrated Tactical Planning for senior executives to understand the fundamentals so they can inspire their teams with the knowledge of its effectiveness and maybe identify the missing ingredient in truly freeing up management's time to spend more of it on strategy and other value-add activities. People who are in planning roles will also find it useful, especially if they are frustrated and struggling to get cross-functional buy-in to what they know needs to be improved. This book will reveal concepts that have been shown to work across a range of industries and sizes of organization.

Demystifying Terminology

The sales and operations planning (S&OP) process has had a massive impact on business since Oliver Wight first introduced it in the 1980s. In the early days, S&OP was designed to align the Sales outlook with the Production plan and resulting inventory. As one consultant back then was noted saying, "It is designed to stop the 'blood on the conference room floor' caused by the misalignment and misunderstanding of perspectives, when sales and operations people get together to prioritize plans."

S&OP has become the standard for defining a robust monthly management framework that brings together often-competing plans, perspectives, and goals. The fundamentals introduced by Oliver Wight, such as, "one set of integrated plans and numbers," being the "decision-making forum for the business," "*management by exception*," and "bad news early is better than bad news late," have stood the test of time.

More recently S&OP has evolved to be known as Integrated Business Planning, which is designed to include all other plans and functions that were not initially included in S&OP. It now truly does integrate all plans and functions in a business and is seen as *the* management process for running a business, big or small. It includes product and portfolio management, financial evaluation of the plans, and, most important, alignment with strategy. Indeed, you could argue that the modern version of Integrated Business Planning is designed to operationalize strategy.

The terminology in this book may be a bit daunting if you've not experienced an S&OP or Integrated Business Planning process before, not to mention the myriad technical terms used in the planning and supporting processes. Therefore, we have included a glossary at the end of this book, and the APICS Dictionary is also a good source of information about standard processes and terms.

If you are familiar with the term *S&OP*, we'll be using Integrated Business Planning from here on, and although they are not 100% interchangeable, for the purpose of this book, we'll assume that it means the monthly management framework. We will explain a little more in Chapter 2 but have intentionally kept references and descriptions of Integrated Business Planning to a minimum, because this book is about Integrated Tactical Planning.

The Rationale

There has been something missing from the monthly management process that has, in many cases, suboptimized the outcomes, which is, how to aggregate longer-range plans and align them with what is being done day to day? One of the hallmarks of Integrated Business Planning is that it is designed to focus on the mid- to longer term of at least 24 months. So, who is looking after the short term? These are time-critical issues and processes, but if you have designed only a monthly management process then how does this work? That is where the weekly Integrated Tactical Planning process fits in.

It is a change in mindset. Rather than create a great plan out in the future and then "hope and pray" that it actually happens, the Integrated Tactical Planning process will take said plan with both hands, watch over it, respond to its needs, and then deliver it safely to execution. Another Oliver Wight truism, which is relevant here, is "silence is approval." This means that if senior management doesn't hear anything, then they can safely assume that everything is still on track.

The Benefits

One of the most notable differences between a monthly planning process and a weekly planning process is obviously cadence. If you're running it weekly, each year there are 52 improvement opportunities, as opposed to 12 at most for a monthly process. From start-up of Integrated Tactical Planning to the delivery of sustained improvements in performance metrics, working capital, and cross-functional teamwork can be as quick as 12 weeks. In fact, many of our clients tell us that they start getting benefits in the first 4 weeks. One process lead at an agri-business company commented, "The sales lead loves the new process because it has eliminated at least 12 phone calls a day, and the gap we identified 4 weeks ago between the demand plan and the projected harvest volumes allowed us to purchase from other suppliers early and closed the supply gap cost-effectively." Integrated Tactical Planning helps foster confidence in execution and credibility from customers who view the organization as a reliable partner.

Of course, if there is only the weekly Integrated Tactical Planning process without the longer horizon monthly process, ultimately, there will be a loss of direction and connection to direction setting and strategic trade-offs, so both monthly and weekly processes are needed. It is, however, important to recognize that they have very different purposes and objectives. On a final note, some companies have tried to blend both weekly and monthly processes into one, by running a weekly S&OP process or breaking their monthly numbers into weeks. This doesn't work. Just from a purely numbers perspective, it more than quadruples the number of data points and creates a level of detail that is often unworkable. It often causes people to drop the long-term view or aggregate the short-term numbers to too high a level to properly see the issues.

Acknowledgments

This book would not have been possible without the dedication of a number of people. The Oliver Wight International Board is to be thanked for seeing the value of elevating the understanding and awareness of the Integrated Tactical Planning process and approving the plans for publication of this book. The following people were particularly instrumental:

- Rod Hozack for doing the background research, identifying the gap in our offerings to clients, and sparking the concept for further development; he also brings a wealth of experience in product and portfolio management and strategy deployment
- Stuart Harman for being the co-developer of the process in Asia Pacific and bringing his experience of performance measurement and continuous improvement
- Todd Ferguson for seeing the vision and possibilities and bringing his depth of knowledge in demand planning, execution, and forecasting
- Dawn Howarth for bringing her deep understanding of operations, manufacturing, supply chain, and her brilliance in editing the copy down to be truly focused and razor sharp

CHAPTER 1

Great Execution

An Overview

Do you ever feel that your business signs off on a solid plan every month, but it is never actually delivered? Does everyone seem to be running around putting out the latest fire, crashing from one crisis to another, but thinking that each one is an isolated incident that could not have been predicted? Is your team stressed out with trying to keep their heads above water with all of these changes so that they never actually have any time to work on long-term fixes for problems and only ever apply a bandage before moving on to the next fire? Or is everyone looking over everyone else's shoulder to make sure that things are done because they either don't trust them to do things or don't really know who should be doing what?

If you feel any of these symptoms apply to you, then read on.

Most businesses now have some form of a monthly planning process that looks to balance supply and *demand* over at least the current year. This type of process started life as sales and operations planning (S&OP), but Oliver Wight evolved it into what is now known as *Integrated Business Planning*. What many businesses don't appreciate is that this type of process is fine for the mid- to long-term future to identify and address the gaps in strategy and *business plans*, but in the short term you need a complementary suite of processes with more frequent cadence and more granularity of detail to actually make the monthly plan happen. This is called *Integrated Tactical Planning*.

The value of a good planning environment is not so much about the planning capability, but as Oliver Wight put it more than 40 years ago, it is the ability to "re-predict, re-predict, re-predict" (Wight, 1981). In modern parlance, that means a formal planning environment that has the ability to replan quickly and accurately as circumstances change and engage the right people, at the right level, in the right time *horizon*, to collaboratively agree to the change in plans.

Having said that, businesses need a good plan to start with, so we are not suggesting this is a replacement for a rock-solid Integrated Business Planning process looking out for the next 2 to 3 years, but what we are suggesting is that change is inevitable, and the Integrated Business Planning process should not be managing those changes in the next 3 months. What companies need is a robust lower-level process, with the purpose of rebalancing plans each week to meet the Integrated Business Planning plan in the next 3 months . . . and if it can't be done, they need to communicate that fact early.

The key to why Integrated Tactical Planning is crucial to running a business well is summarized in the following three ingredients that explain why some companies make it and others don't:

1. Reducing the time it takes the executive team to manage the business (operational activities) by a factor of five
2. Refocusing the executive team on market-facing activities
3. Realigning everyone else (onto the same page) to drive execution and results

Integrated Tactical Planning in concert with Integrated Business Planning is a fundamental process that provides businesses with the confidence that these objectives will be met.

Introduction

Welcome to the well-hidden world of the Integrated Tactical Planning process. In a sea of advice from consultants and subject matter experts on the monthly business-management framework of Integrated Business Planning, there are very few references as to how the Integrated Business Planning process plans get deployed. (If you are not familiar with the concept of Integrated Business Planning process, Chapter 2 will expand the concept a little further and its relevance to the layers of business planning.) The Integrated Tactical Planning process is the heartbeat or control tower of execution in a business, and the intent of this book is to reorientate your way of thinking about the differences among the layers of planning and the differences between planning and execution.

If you feel like the executive team is continually being sucked into managing immediate and urgent issues, and other senior managers don't seem to be able to break out of focusing on the next few months (at best),

FIGURE 1.1 Wildfire

and there's very little confidence in predicting the end-of-year position, it is likely you need greater discipline in getting the tactical horizon under control. As one senior executive was heard saying, "It feels like there's a wildfire burning unpredictably, and we just can't get ahead of it to create a fire break. Even if we did get ahead of it, we wouldn't know where to put it!" (See Figure 1.1.)

If this sounds like your company, it is not hard to get started, and once started, the benefits will come quickly. Excuse the pun, but you just need to create the "burning platform" for the business and get going, and then you need to structure a *sustainability plan* so it becomes self-perpetuating.

About the Process

This book will give you the basic definitions, concepts, and real-life examples of how Integrated Tactical Planning has been applied in various industries and businesses, and, importantly, give you enough information to help your organization get started. It is, however, not the definitive text on the subject. By the end, though, you will understand enough about the concepts and application to know that taking a cookie-cutter approach will not work. Process design must be aligned with your company structure, its strategy, and its go-to-market approach, and you must recognize that behavior and culture are highly likely to need to change.

Why Integrated Tactical Planning?

Although this is not a new concept, it has not had much airplay over the last couple of decades because it has been overshadowed by a growing understanding and desire to deploy mid- to long-term aggregate planning processes (Integrated Business Planning) in businesses. This monthly management framework has delivered enormous benefits to businesses, but in some circumstances, it has led to a blurring of objectives between a monthly senior management planning process and the weekly middle-management execution of those plans. When we say, "execution of those plans," we usually mean the next 3 months, but we'll cover how to determine the time frame later in the book.

Many Integrated Business Planning processes struggle to focus enough time on the longer term because the shorter-term (tactical) issues keep getting in the way. In the 50 years that Oliver Wight has been helping companies run better businesses, we don't know of any examples of companies that have too many resources to do what needs to get done, and hence, the focus is on having the right level of people in the organization, making the right decisions, on the rights things, at the right time.

The other symptom we often see is a gulf between the monthly medium- to long-range planning process and execution of those plans in the next week or so, with nothing in between. When we started working with a food company recently, they ran a rudimental monthly Integrated Business Planning process, and the only process thereafter was a daily sales and supply schedule check. By putting off considering some of the materials they needed to purchase 12 to 14 weeks out, it left purchasing second-guessing most of their purchases. They ended up with either holding too much raw and packaging materials or running out of critical ingredients. It also meant that there was no way to use the planning system to manage purchases. This expensive piece of planning software just became a transactional system—and is such a *waste* of resources both human and computer.

To contextualize where Integrated Tactical Planning fits, there are five fundamental levels of planning (see Figure 1.2):

1. Annual strategic and business planning processes—typically a horizon of 5 to 10 years
2. Quarterly check-ins to the strategic themes, key metrics review, and the cost of the go-to-market approach
3. Monthly realignment with the annual business and strategic planning horizons—typically a horizon of a rolling 24 months, but 36 months is becoming more common (the Integrated Business Planning process)

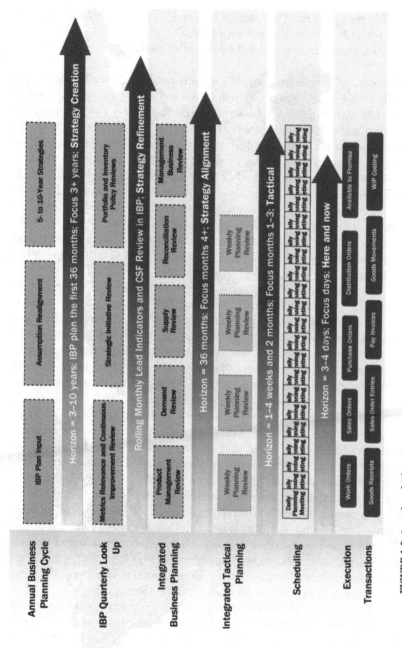

FIGURE 1.2 Levels of Planning

Source: Oliver Wight. Copyright Oliver Wight International, Inc. Used with permission.

4. Weekly realignment of the tactical horizon back to the monthly horizon (the Integrated Tactical Planning process)
5. Daily execution and alignment back to the weekly plan

This book will cover primarily the weekly process shown in point 4, but ultimately best-in-class businesses will have one set of plans that cut across each level of planning. This is, however, where confusion and misalignment can occur. One client, who exported perishable items around the world, was quite specific about the break in integration with the comment, "We put a lot of effort into doing our monthly management process and making sure the numbers and plans are aligned out to 36 months, but then immediately after we sign them off, we forget about them until next month, and wonder why we never hit our plans." The moral of this story is that to create greater certainty in delivering our plans, from strategy to daily execution, we need mechanisms to ensure congruence across all levels of planning and execution and the ability to realign—top to bottom, and bottom to top—when things change.

Integrated Tactical Planning is the suite of processes that ensures alignment between the monthly plan, and what is done day-to-day. Many of our clients have demonstrated results with Integrated Tactical Planning very quickly, but in order for complete alignment with strategy, Integrated Tactical Planning also needs to be aligned with long-range plans generated from a robust Integrated Business Planning process, which takes its guidance from strategy. The result is an aligned set of plans and numbers that is designed to deliver sustained competitive advantage.

Think of it like a bicycle road race, such as the Tour de France, where there is a route that is set ahead of time. All the competitors will be aware of the route, would have studied it, and probably would have driven and ridden it many times in the lead-up to the race. There is, however, still a lead motorcycle to show the way. Why? Because the cyclists are so engrossed in what they are doing in the moment that there is precious little bandwidth left to think big picture about the overall route, let alone which turns to make and when—once racing, the plan is set, and they are now in tactical execution. There will be bumps along the way, such as flat tires, falls and injuries, illness, rain, spectators, and more; most of which will have been considered and contingency plans formulated, but each will need to be managed as they occur in a tactical sense to stay on track with the overall plan.

As a supply chain director said to us in the early days of working with his company, "We don't need this cadence and congruence stuff; we pay people to react and be flexible, and formality and discipline just get in the way." To a certain extent, there is logic in that argument. If we had absolute certainty on the outcomes of all our plans, we would not need any of these layers of process. The key, however, is to understand that *plans are going to change,* and it is how we respond to change that is the real value—it is the difference between reacting and responding. Reacting involves no anticipation or planning, and responding is the opposite—the what-if question has been asked prior, and a set of premeditated contingency plans formulated in readiness. So, assuming that you have a good plan to start with, it is not the planning that is important, it is the replanning and anticipation of change that counts more.

When changes to plans do occur, those plans need to be continually realigned back to the overall direction. That is what we call *closed-loop* planning systems, where at any one time we know we have congruent plans from the big picture right down to what is being actioned right now.

Integrated Tactical Planning Rationale

The key difference an Integrated Tactical Planning process brings to the business is that it is deliberately designed to be a weekly cross-functional replanning process, with the specific intent of rebalancing plans back up to the Integrated Business Planning process plans inside the tactical horizon.

The process relies on key roles being defined and those roles then being responsible for actively managing changes to *core plans* inside the tactical window (which will vary from company to company, and a formal definition will be shared in Chapter 2). Think of core plans as the product portfolio plan, the *demand plan,* and the supply plan. These are the input plans, and all other plans are outputs from these plans; for example, an inventory plan is an output of the balance between the demand plan and the supply plan.

The issue that Integrated Tactical Planning solves in the tactical horizon is the many-to-many communication needs. In a good Integrated Tactical Planning process, a cross-functional *quorum* of people is assigned to proactively seek, manage, and communicate changes to plans. Organizations can also exacerbate the chaos caused by the many-to-many communication by allowing information to get trapped in functional silos. This can happen even in smaller organizations, so can you imagine how the complexity exponentially increases in organizations with tens of thousands of people in multiple locations.

A simple equation to highlight this is (n^2-n), where n is the number of people in an organization, and when you solve this equation, it is the number of possible communication permutations at any point in time. Now add in, email communications, corridor conversations, meeting actions, the lunchroom conversations, and more, and it doesn't take long to see that this is an exponential curve as depicted in Figure 1.3.

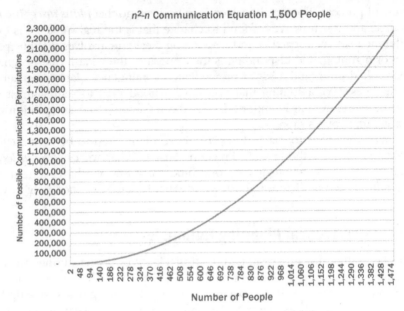

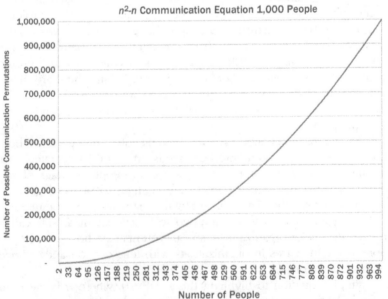

FIGURE 1.3 Number of Communication Permutations

Source: Oliver Wight. Copyright Oliver Wight International, Inc. Used with permission.

To give you a few numbers: if we had 10 people in an organization, the number of communication permutations at any one time is 90. This is eminently manageable. If we have 100 people, the number of communication permutations is 9,900, which becomes more of a juggle. If you were in a mid-sized organization of 500 to 1,500 people, the number of communication permutations becomes huge—249,500 and 2,248,500, respectively. How do you manage that much communication? Without a framework, you don't! One of the early ways to manage this was through functions and a command-and-control management style. As mentioned previously, all that does is trap information in functions, departments, regions, sites, or any other structural boundaries organizations tend to create to control outcomes.

The only way to manage this in a cross-functional and whole-of-business way is to create a structure of formal communication and decision-making, which we call Integrated Business Planning and Integrated Tactical Planning processes, and, yes, they are decision-making and action-oriented processes. If your meetings are more or less information sharing and talk fests, you're missing an *opportunity*.

A starting point we often use with clients is to spend time understanding what decisions are made, at what level in the organization, and in what time horizon, and then assign those decisions to the relevant layer in the planning process. In this case, decisions about rebalancing plans every week and reconciling back to the signed-off Integrated Business Planning process plans lie with the Integrated Tactical Planning process. As an aside, this then assists with defining the *escalation criteria*, which is activated if plans cannot be rebalanced within agreed tolerances and time frames, and requires a definition of process and roles to effectively resolve the imbalances. The intent should be to design the process so that those who enact the changes are authorized to make the required decisions. There are times, however, when the cost and/or the impact of the change is so great that a higher level of authority needs to be engaged. People need guidance to know when that threshold is about to be breached and then how to go about getting authorization to resolve.

The first step is to define the key roles, or quorum. The role definitions need to be written in such a way as to authorize these people to proactively identify changes to core plans and assess whether that change *will actually become* a problem. Note, the tense in the previous sentence is future tense; an important behavioral characteristic is to anticipate potential issues in the tactical horizon, with the objective to eliminate surprises.

Also, the bigger the organization, the more deliberate and formal the nodes of information collation and decision-making need to be. The many-to-many communication, and/or hierarchical escalation, is just too time-consuming and human resource hungry to profitably survive in this modern world.

The quorum then owns the management of core plans in the tactical horizon (core plans being the product portfolio, demand, and supply plans). The group proactively seeks out changes and follows a predefined decision-making and escalation set of criteria questions, or RACI (a role-definition template whose name stands for **r**esponsible, **a**ccountable, **c**onsulted, **i**nformed):

- Who wants to make the change?
- What is the cost of the change?
- Does the change affect other areas or functions?
- What are the options for resolution?
- What is the recommended approach?
- Is the benefit of making the change greater than the cost of doing the change?
- Who needs to sign off on the change?
- Who needs to know about the decision?
- Should we have seen the need for this change earlier?

Another important business principle bigger than just Integrated Tactical Planning is that the process must be set up to foster learning so that over time the gray areas of decision-making become more precisely defined and understood. An indication that the learning is being effectively wound back into process is through stability (a reduction in the number of plan changes within certain time frames), reductions in numbers of escalations, and reductions in physical constraints, such as reducing *time fences* and flexibility measures. In the beginning there are usually a lot of changes occurring, which is often referred to as "nervous planning," but as time goes on, the number of changes decrease, and a calmness develops in managing the small number of changes that do occur.

Integrating the Business: The Maturity Journey

Maturity maps have become more widespread in recent years, but few people know how to use them. Everyone would like their businesses to be totally seamless and integrated with technology (see Phase 4 in Figure 1.4), but what is usually missed is mapping out the journey up through the phases. We often refer to this as an investment model, in that there are certain things that need to be in place to act as foundations and building blocks to facilitate the next phase of performance.

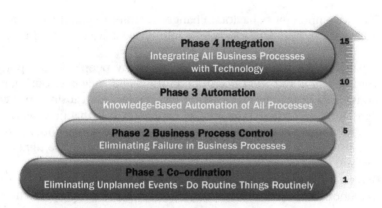

FIGURE 1.4 Business Excellence Maturity Chart

Source: Oliver Wight. Copyright Oliver Wight International, Inc. Used with permission.

Oliver Wight uses maturity maps to plot the journey up through the phases to assess where and when to allocate or invest resources to evolve to a higher level of maturity. This is explained in more detail in *The Oliver Wight Class A Standard for Business Excellence* (Oliver Wight International, 2017), but it is worth briefly positioning the Integrated Tactical Planning process within the maturity context.

As mentioned previously, most companies aspire to be operating at Phase 4 when all business processes are integrated with technology. However, many companies have spent a lot of money on technology only to have a small percentage of that investment realized. The reason is that to get to Phase 4, the company needs to go through a journey from Phase 1 through Phase 3; you can't jump steps. A fundamental process in Phase 1 is the Integrated Tactical Planning process. Without it, the company is going to struggle to mature into Phase 2.

Phase 1 is characterized by working to eliminate the unplanned events that we talked about in the opening paragraphs and doing the routine things routinely to develop the structure and cadence to manage the business in a more controlled manner. There are behavioral, process, and technology elements to be addressed to get to the top of Phase 1. Behavior is often the most difficult to address in that this is a new way of working for many, and it is likely to challenge many long-held beliefs and ingrained ways of working. We don't actually mean unplanned events are literally eliminated. They will, however, be fewer and be more effectively managed when they do occur. As one operations manager aptly described it, "It's amazing how many unplanned events you can actually plan for!"

The two important behavioral changes that are required to get to the top of Phase 1 and prepare for moving into Phase 2 are described here:

A passion for data integrity. Not too many people would put the words *passion* and *data accuracy* in the same sentence, but there is always a lot of passion expressed if inaccuracies are causing erroneous plans and information. Data are like feral animals in that they need taming and training, and not just as a one-off exercise. Once under control, data just need a gentle hand to continually steer them in the right direction and keep on track.

Driven by process. Focus, discipline, and a never-ending drive for continuous improvement are key characteristics of high performance. It doesn't matter whether it is becoming a musician, an elite athlete, or a market-leading business, without these qualities, businesses will eventually wither and die.

As mentioned, most people do not get excited about process adherence, 100% data accuracy, or carving out time for doing root cause analysis and creating a *corrective-action plan*. It takes time, and it requires discipline and some hard thinking. If, however, we want to make the system work and create certainty in planning and execution, it is fundamental to be done. The benefits are a reduction in the amount of noise in planning and the ability to use the system to keep all planning levels congruent all the time. The benefits of one set of plans and numbers that everyone trusts and works toward can't be overstated.

To support this, however, technology needs to be considered early in the design and deployment phase. Although not recommended, many processes can be driven by a spreadsheet in Phase 1, but as processes mature, and the business becomes more certain about doing the routine things routinely, fit-for-purpose software and tools are going to be required. This is how the maturity journey becomes an investment model to ensure processes are supported by appropriate technology at the right time . . . and not before. As the CEO of a very large retail company once said, "Don't talk to me about software; we have purchased so much software in the past, and none of it is being used, and worse still, much of it is still unwrapped in the box it came in!"

The other question to ask about technology is, "What do you already have?" We usually get strange looks, but on further investigation, we will usually find that several modules were purchased in the original *enterprise resource planning (ERP)* implementation but aren't being used. Worse still, there is no one who knows how to use them, and sometimes it's been so long that there is no corporate memory of what was originally purchased.

But remember, a tool is seldom the answer in isolation. You need to be clear as to what you want it to do for you and how you are going to use it before you invest or even before you dust off the cobwebs of something you already have.

Do We Know What Game We Are Playing?

Our go-to-market approach is critical for maintaining a company's competitive edge, but all too often when asked, most people in *supply chain* and operations would say they have a good working model of their supply chain, but the knowledge gets a bit more fragmented and sketchy as people from other departments are quizzed. As a supply chain director once quipped, "Why do they need to know?" The answer is straightforward, and that is, if running a viable business is about getting our products to our consumers—at the right time, at the right price, and with expected quality—then understanding the supply chain and its inherent peculiarities, limitations, and costs is critical for everyone to understand and can have a profound impact on competitiveness if not well understood.

As an example, that same supply chain director came back to us after he and a cross-functional team had spent considerable time mapping out their many supply chains and said, "I can't believe it. We have at least 27 distinct supply chains, eight manufacturing sites, 83 stocking points around the country—three of which I didn't know about—and a lot of missing steps and missing control points in the *routing*. No wonder we can't get this under control!"

One of the prerequisites of Integrated Tactical Planning is to map out the supply chain as it exists today to understand the scope and scale of the world your company operates in to at least our most immediate suppliers and customers—referred to as tier-1 customers and tier-1 suppliers in Figure 1.5. Although it is implicit that this should also include our segmented go-to-market approach, it is important to emphasis this point to make sure we engage marketing and sales in the understanding and leveraging the current supply chain. This will not only assist in deciding how to structure the Integrated Tactical Planning process but also it will lead to highlighting areas for improvement in supply chain capability and overall business profitability. Our experience as practitioners suggests there is a significant opportunity in the marketplace for increased cross-functional collaboration—driven by strategy through Integrated Business Planning and monitored for execution in Integrated Tactical Planning.

The parameters noted in Figure 1.5 are a subset of what could be a large set of supply chain parameters and variables, but for the intent of the Integrated Tactical Planning process, these are the key parameters. A recent

		TIER 1 SUPPLIERS	PRIMARY PRODUCTION	SECONDARY PRODUCTION	WAREHOUSING AND DISTRIBUTION	TIER 1 CUSTOMERS
Customers/ Channels	No. of customers/orders per day/week Complexity of orders (H/M/L) Demand lead time—receipt to ship					
NPD/NPI activity	Frequency of Activity Significance to Portfolio					
Internal Suppliers	Number of interdependencies Visibility of planning between nodes					
Distribution Points	Number of supply points World areas/lead times					
Known constraints	Space/cash/capacity/people or skills?					
Key Relationships	Who are the key players in the supply chain?					
Supply Response Time	Where do you meet your customer (MTS/MTO)					

FIGURE 1.5 Understanding Your Supply Chains

Note: NPD: new product development; NPI: new product introduction; MTS: make to stock; MTO: make to order.

Source: Oliver Wight. Copyright Oliver Wight International, Inc. Used with permission.

client's supply chain director took this a step further and started planning out a number of improvement initiatives at each supply point, then created a visual representation that he pasted up on one wall of his office. There was no way you could miss it.

The initiatives were designed to align with addressing each of the following elements:

- People and behavior
- Process design and integrity that marries people's knowledge of the business with Oliver Wight's definition of best-practice integration
- Tools and technology application and use aligned with the company's level of maturity
- Metrics and the improvement framework that covered data integrity, process delivery, and strategic improvements

The initiatives could be simple, such as, running a best-practice education session for a key supplier, to formalizing data-sharing protocols between two *supply points*, right through to a complex program to remove all the data-holding and planning spreadsheets and replace them with the ERP system modules, which touches on all the key elements of change management (people and behavior, process, tools, and metrics).

Aligning Systems with Planning

As mentioned, there is a chronology of elements to effectively creating change (see Figure 1.6). First, we need to make sure people have a good understanding of the concepts, the vision of what excellence looks like, and the knowledge of what is required of them. Second, we need to engage those people in the design of process and deployment plans so that processes support their specific organization. Finally, we can then align tools and technology requirements with the new process to effectively support both people and process. This then becomes a never-ending upward spiral of ensuring the business continues its journey up the maturity chart by investing in the right tools and technology at the right time.

In Phase 1, organizations need to match the technology with the immediate and near-future level of maturity, and in most instances that translates to using the planning modules in an ERP system to facilitate process, effectively manage the integrity of the data, and assist with making people's working lives easier. Virtually all ERP planning systems are based on the same *materials requirements planning (MRP)* logic, and even if the business is not a manufacturing organization, the ERP logic still works to integrate demand planning with supply and inventory planning, as well as the aggregating financial projections, which often get forgotten.

The data coming out of a well-set-up ERP planning system are all that are necessary to effectively feed the Integrated Business Planning process, the Integrated Tactical Planning process, and day-to-day monitoring and

FIGURE 1.6 A Simple but Powerful Change Model

Source: Oliver Wight. Copyright Oliver Wight International, Inc. Used with permission.

execution of these plans. There is obviously more to it, but the point is that if processes are well defined and adhered to, then the right technology can make a world of difference.

There is an argument that spreadsheets can manage well enough in a less sophisticated planning environment, but when a company's processes evolve even just a little beyond basic planning, the availability of an integrated set of data using modern systems can offer real-time information, instant simulation capability, and a whole lot more in the way of analytics, *optimization*, and predictive capability. If, however, the underlying processes are less than robust and people's knowledge of what excellent looks like is poor, then no amount of technology is going to help. Even today, there's no computer planning system that can handle an informal and ad hoc environment.

Summary and Key Change Requirements

The Integrated Tactical Planning process is a weekly cross-functional replanning process with a horizon covering the tactical horizon of the business. Its primary purpose is to proactively seek out changes to core plans and rebalance those plans back to the plans that were signed off in the most recent Integrated Business Planning cycle. It is a core element of Phase 1 business maturity and relies on fundamental information coming from an enterprise-quality set of planning modules.

Being a weekly cadence, benefits come quickly, versus the monthly Integrated Business Planning process, which by its nature of a monthly cycle takes longer to be embedded and deliver results. It is, however, important to emphasize that Integrated Tactical Planning will not eliminate the need for longer horizon plans. Direction is important, and as the old saying goes, "Without a destination, any road will get you there."

PEOPLE AND BEHAVIOR CHANGES
- Senior management need to be engaged in process design with the objective of leading deployment and then stepping away to spend more time on the longer term horizon.
- The next level of management needs to be empowered to run the Integrated Tactical Planning process and escalate only by exception.

PROCESS CHANGES
- The intent of the Integrated Tactical Planning process is to deliver the Integrated Business Management process plans inside the tactical horizon.
- Focus is on the core input plans—demand, supply, and product; all other plans are outputs.

TECHNOLOGY CHANGES
- Use the system planning modules.
- Have a strategic intent to eliminate data-holding and planning spreadsheets.
- Develop a passion for data integrity, process integrity, and having the whole business working to one set of operational plans and numbers.

In the following chapters, we will dive deeper into these core principles and build the foundations for running and maintaining a robust Integrated Tactical Planning process.

CHAPTER 2

Empowering the Organization

Core Disciplines That Set Companies Apart

The Integrated Business Planning process sits at the heart of the *Integrated Business Model* (see Figure 2.1) and is the glue that holds everything together. It is a monthly aggregate business-planning process that is designed to keep senior managers focused on a horizon of 4 to 36 months and its alignment with the strategic plan horizon.

The Integrated Business Model

The nine elements of a business, as described in the *Oliver Wight Class A Standard for Business Excellence* (7th ed.), are listed below. We need to make sure all are well defined and working effectively. The Integrated Business Planning process is designed to realign core plans with the strategic aspirations of the business and is an aggregate business planning process, often known as *above the line*, Integrated Tactical Planning is designed to operate at a more granular level of detail, with the objective to realign plans weekly in the tactical horizon back to the latest signed-off monthly plan. This is what we call *below the line* in Figure 2.1, referring to the 10 underpinnings and more detailed-level processes that are constantly running in the background:

1. Managing the Strategic Planning Process.
2. Managing and Leading People.
3. Driving Business Improvement.
4. Integrated Business Planning.
5. Managing Products and Services.
6. Managing Demand.

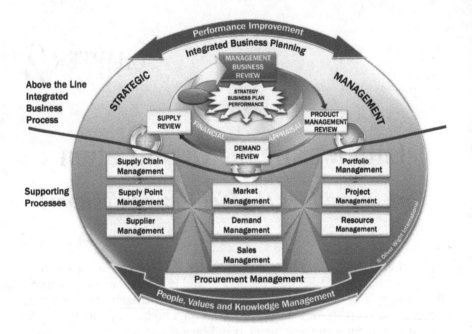

FIGURE 2.1 The Integrated Business Model

Source: Oliver Wight. Copyright Oliver Wight International, Inc. Used with permission.

7. Managing the Supply Chain.
8. Managing Internal Supply.
9. Managing External Sourcing.

So, although Integrated Business Planning is about realigning plans back to strategy on a monthly basis and integrating all elements in the business, the Integrated Tactical Planning process is about living Oliver Wight's aspiration of "silence is approval." This means, if senior management don't hear anything to the contrary, then they should assume that everything is still on plan. This is a long way off in many businesses we work with in that it is almost a badge of honor for senior managers to be meddling in the detail and managing crises on a daily basis.

There are, however, fundamental concepts and mechanics that need to be in place to make this work effectively. We see these fundamental concepts as the basics in business, but it is surprising just how many senior managers don't know them or pay scant attention. Yet, without them, uncertainty and chaos are likely to arise on a daily basis. The following describes these fundamental concepts:

Time fences are the rules for managing changes to plans. As we get closer to today, it becomes more expensive and disruptive to change plans and hence requires a more disciplined approach to making changes to plans in general.

The **quorum** comprises key roles defined to own core plans and form nodes of communication and issue management, which then minimizes the chaos that results from the many-to-many management of issues.

Understand the *Pareto principle* and the lore of Managing the Vital Few. Prioritize the *customer promise* in which all customers and products are not necessarily treated equal.

Use effective escalation criteria and communication.

Demonstrated capability is the use of known performance as the starting point for creating plans. It avoids setting plans up to fail.

Manage uncertainty through *scenario planning*.

Recognize **change management** as an everyday management practice. People don't easily accept change in organizations and every process change needs a change plan to help bring people along with the required changes.

We will cover these in more detail next, then tease out the next level of detail of the core plans and the overall process in subsequent chapters.

Time Fences

Time fences are one of the most important and yet most poorly applied principles we have seen in business. A simple way to put it is that there are the physical reaction times the organization has to work with to make effective decisions. A simple example is one of the fundamental principles for people first learning to drive a car, and that is the 3-second rule. This means keeping 3 seconds of space behind the car in front of you to allow for things going wrong, which in this case, is allowing for people's physical reaction time. The best race car drivers can get their reaction time down to 0.3 seconds, but for the rest of us it is about 1 second, and if we don't drive very often, we may even struggle to hit the 2-second target. Then think about what that means if you're travelling at; say; 60 mph. The Formula 1 driver will take just 0.3 seconds to respond, which is less than 27 feet. One second translates to covering 88 feet before reacting, and 2 seconds equates to having covered 176 feet by the time your foot hits the brake pedal.

Alternatively, you can drive very close to the person in front, as some drivers do, and get away with it for a while. Eventually however, you will come unstuck. Some leaders will say, "In business we're like athletes and should be aiming for the 0.3 second reaction time." Consider what the preparation and dedication is for a Formula 1 race car driver—training every day in the gym, using simulators, and performing speed tests—and the years they have spent working their way up through the ranks from go-carts to the fastest cars on the track. If you're prepared to put the organization on the treadmill for excellence, then we'd be all for it. In the interim, while the organization is making those improvements, we need to set time fences to what the reality is right here and now. As the road safety campaigns would say, "Only a fool breaks the 3-second rule."

The key time fence for Integrated Tactical Planning is what we refer to as the planning time fence (PTF). In a planning system sense, this is the horizon in which we recommend people must take control of the plans, with the computer operating in a supporting role. The default position is to define the PTF from the time a purchase order is released for the longest *lead time* material through to a finished product being available for shipment or sale to a customer (see Figure 2.2). This is referred to as the *cumulative lead time*, and it defines the response time for the business to make changes if usual rules and lead times are followed. Within this period we know we have to make choices and decisions because not everything is possible. As one company described it, "To respond quicker means we got lucky; do you want to plan your business on always being lucky?"

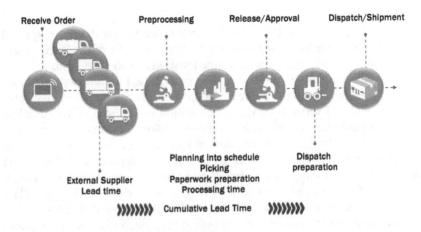

FIGURE 2.2 Cumulative Lead Time Calculation

Source: Oliver Wight. Copyright Oliver Wight International, Inc. Used with permission.

This does not just apply to a manufacturing business, either. In a supply chain organization, it would still be defined as the time to procure finished goods, and if you take the suppliers' capabilities into account, the lead times usually end up being roughly the same or even longer than those producing their own goods.

There are essentially two key reason behind defining time fences for the Integrated Tactical Planning process:

1. **Drive focus and ownership of the different time horizons.** As noted in Figure 2.3, the Integrated Business Planning process is projecting out well beyond the PTF and assumes that change outside this time will come at no or little cost and will be physically possible. The decisions in this time period are often more strategic, and you can take more time in considering them.

2. **Critical business** *decision points.* Inside the PTF, the organization has already committed to spending money, and hence any changes inside that time is going to cost something. The closer we get to today, the more it is going to cost to change plans; for example, we might have to airfreight items, run an overtime shift, or cut a customer order short. We also have less time to respond to these changes, so we need to monitor things more closely and respond more quickly when these changes occur.

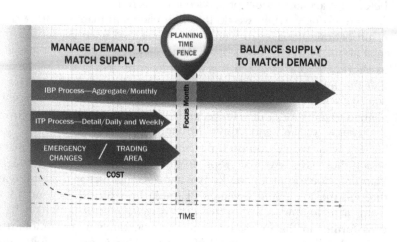

FIGURE 2.3 PTF and Focus Month

Source: Oliver Wight. Copyright Oliver Wight International, Inc. Used with permission.

This change in horizon and behavior is referred to as the *focus month*, and as the CEO of one of our companies would often say, "It is the difference between what we think we're going to do, and what we *will* be doing."

We therefore recommend having at least a 13-week horizon for the Integrated Tactical Planning process, even if the PTF analysis comes in at less than 13 weeks. This is because we want to ensure that the Integrated Business Planning process has a focus on months 4 to 36, with the shorter-term execution horizon, being effectively managed through the weekly Integrated Tactical Planning process.

In defining the first key reason, there is no real science in defining 13 weeks, except that we want a different group of people managing the shorter term and with a different purpose, which is to be responsible for delivering the first 3 months of the Integrated Business Planning process plan or communicate otherwise . . . and as early as possible. The intent is that it's better to have bad news early than bad news late.

We sometimes get asked about how this might work in a service industry, and in those types of businesses, the question to answer is, "How long would it take to acquire the appropriate resource to be able to cost-effectively deliver to a change in customer requirements?" In professional services firms, such as law, accounting, and medical, key resource acquisition could be several months, but the point remains that even in nonphysical goods environments, there will still be a lead or reaction time to source critical resources that will cost the business money at some point in time before the actual product or service is delivered.

Interestingly, when we do this with clients in manufacturing or supply chain organizations, even with overseas-sourced material, it usually comes in at about 13 weeks, occasionally 15 to 18 weeks, and sometimes it can be as short as 4 to 8 weeks. If it is a shorter time period, we still recommend that the Integrated Tactical Planning horizon be set at 13 weeks to make sure we cover point 1. The formal plan-change process, however, might be aligned to the shorter time fence, and out to 13 weeks would be covered by the weekly demand and supply rebalancing process.

So, what would you do if the business was an agricultural business in which they have seasonal crops? In this case, keep the Integrated Tactical Planning horizon at 13 weeks but manage the seasonal supply variation through the integrated Business Planning horizon out beyond 13 weeks, using a technique called *rough-cut capacity planning*, which we'll discuss further in the Chapter 5. This then becomes a consumption model in which the demand is netted off against a projection of finite supply at an aggregate level beyond 3 months. The thinking is exactly the same as if the company was modeling a rate-limiting machine or finite warehouse storage capability.

However, the reason for keeping it to within approximately 13 to 18 weeks is that the Integrated Tactical Planning process is a detailed planning and execution process, usually at individual item or customer level and in a minimum of weekly, but often daily or even hourly, time buckets. Therefore, the longer the horizon, the more data are needed to generate plans. We need to be mindful of the potential quantity of data that could be generated with little extra gain. There are examples of when a whole supply chain is captured in the PTF, such as medical devices, where from sourcing the right base product, creating the component parts, and producing finished goods could be as long as 24 months, and having items travel around the world during that time. This presents a unique problem that we don't have time to go into in this book, but suffice to say, it does require some deeper thinking to get right and to effectively manage longer time fences.

Similar to all calculations and algorithms in business, we like to treat the math as a starting point and then sense check it against knowledge and experience of people in the business. There is no one-size-fits-all solution. Because this is about identifying timing for key decisions, it is worth stating that we often find other critical decisions outside of the supply chain that have longer horizons than the PTF. For example, there may be annual sales contracts that require lengthy negotiations, promotional activity calendars that can be agreed with customers as much as 12 months out, and nearly always a longer time fence for introducing new products. The solution is to ensure that the process definitions for both the Integrated Business Planning process and the Integrated Tactical Planning process are defined and reconciled between the two processes so that there is clear *accountability* for all elements.

There are critical behavioral elements that must be recognized about time fences:

- A time fence is there to make sure that critical decision points are communicated and understood.
- Outside the PTF, the Integrated Business Planning process will rebalance plans at an aggregate monthly level as required.
- Inside the PTF, the Integrated Tactical Planning process will manage changes to meet the commitments and expectations of the Integrated Business Planning process and key policies, such as *order entry*, promising, and inventory.

This doesn't mean that a company should plan to deliver only the forecasted demand without any exceptions. What it means is that we know the future is uncertain, and we should be planning for that uncertainty, which is often called managing to normal-cause variation. This could be using *safety stock*, *safety time*, reserve capacity, or supplier flexibility and would be included in the planning parameters driving the master supply plan.

The important concept is that there is a mechanism to trap changes outside *normal-cause variation* and make sure there is a process to assess not only the doability of the change but also to make sure the cost of the change is less than the benefits that are going to be achieved by making the change. The cost and benefit may not just be a straight-out financial assessment, albeit that is really important; it should also take into account potential disruption to an A customer or a potential miss on a key metric, such as the customer delivery performance or delaying a scheduled maintenance plan.

We'll further explore the use and processes surrounding time fences in Chapters 4 and 5.

The Quorum

In any organization, there are three core plans—product portfolio, demand, and supply—which create other plans, such as the inventory plan, the people plan, and the financial plan. Some might argue that plans such as the financial plan are independent plans, and that is the case in many organizations, but it breaks an Oliver Wight principle of having and working to one set of integrated plans and one set of numbers. Another of the questions we sometimes get is, "Is not the strategic plan a separate plan?" Indeed, it is another level of planning, over potentially an even longer horizon, but product portfolio, demand, and supply plans are still the underpinning plans.

To manage these core plans we need a core group of people. Figure 2.4 shows the primary roles involved in the Integrated Tactical Planning process. It is important to note that these are roles, not necessarily a single person for each role. In a small organization they may overlap and people may wear two hats. In larger organizations, there could be several people doing a similar role. The important point is that the roles are defined.

The *product project manager* is responsible for representing and ensuring the product plans stay on track through the execution phase. The plans would cover activities such as timely inventory builds for launching a new product, ensuring trials and samples that may be required are planned and produced, and that phase-out plans for deleting *stock-keeping units (SKUs)* are well planned and effectively executed.

The *demand manager*/execution manager is responsible for ensuring the demand plan is on track to meet the first 3 months of the demand plan as signed off through last month's Integrated Business Planning process. This would include monitoring sales daily, anticipating and fixing deviations

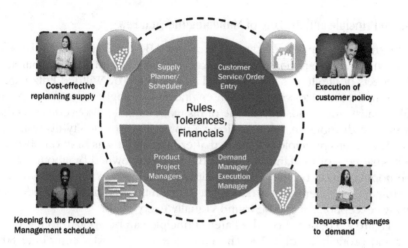

FIGURE 2.4 The Weekly Planning Quorum

Source: Oliver Wight. Copyright Oliver Wight International, Inc. Used with permission.

to the weekly plan, and assessing the knock-on impact of changes to last week's plan to the next 3-month projection.

The *supply planner/scheduler* is responsible for making sure changes to supply plans are made cost-effectively and represent all the supply stakeholders in assessing and managing changes. They too should be looking up each week to make sure they are on track to meet the supply plan as signed off through last-month's Integrated Business Planning cycle.

The fourth role is that of customer service/order entry and that responsibility is to ensure the relationship with the customer and promised orders are aligned with the demand plan. They also own the execution of the customer policy and play a vital role in executing our customer promise in both unconstrained and constrained supply environments. They are the first step in identifying and communicating *abnormal demand* and they execute to the agreed constrained demand plan in times of low supply. They would also be instrumental in other supply or allocation situations, such as managing extraordinary demand prior to a price rise.

The Integrated Tactical Planning process is active and ongoing and culminates in the weekly Integrated Tactical Planning meeting. The important concept to stress is that the quorum is the team of people responsible for proactively identifying potential changes to plans and rebalancing back to the Integrated Business Planning Process plan, whenever possible. When plans cannot be realigned, they are responsible for identifying alternate solutions, seeking authority to change, and communicating and managing the agreed new plan thereafter.

Pareto Principle and the Lore of Managing the Vital Few

Also known as the Power Law, Pareto, and ABC Analysis, this probability distribution curve applies across all facets of business and, for that matter, to all aspects of life. It was first observed and reported by Wilfried Fritz Pareto in the mid-1800s. He was an Italian engineer, sociologist, economist, political scientist, and philosopher. One of his many notable discoveries was that of income distribution, which follows a power law probability distribution.

The Pareto principle was named after him, and it was built on observations that 80% of the land in Italy at the time was owned by about 20% of the population. In business this principle can be seen in the distribution of customers, suppliers, SKUs (stock-keeping units), and although there are always exceptions, it can be found virtually everywhere.

Figure 2.5 depicts how the Pareto principle can be applied to the number and profitability of SKUs. The ratios are 20% of SKUs contribute 80% of the value, 30% of SKUs contribute 15% of the value, and 50% of SKUs contribute just 5% of the total value. In most companies we work with, this distribution curve is approximately prevalent, but more often than not, it is more extreme, such as less than 10% are As, Bs might be 10% to 20%, and Cs 70% to 80%. If an *activity-based costing (ABC)* lens is used across the SKU range, it is common to find that at least half of the C SKUs are losing money.

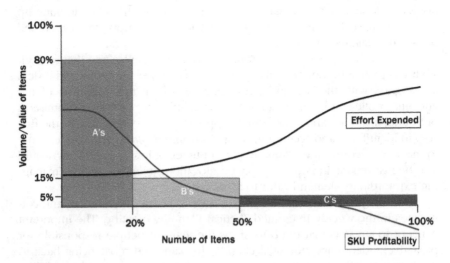

FIGURE 2.5 The Pareto Principle

Source: Oliver Wight. Copyright Oliver Wight International, Inc. Used with permission

On the one hand, a small number of A items is easier to focus on, but also makes the company vulnerable. On the other hand, the cost of managing the C tail can often be huge. Often the sales and marketing team will call foul, in that those C items still contribute some margin. However, this is the problem with only looking at margin and using a standard costing approach. We're not suggesting every company deploy an ABC system, but we do recommend taking an activity-based management approach and understand the weaknesses in the standard costing approach.

So why is the Pareto principle so important to the Integrated Tactical Planning process? It is important for the whole of the business, but particularly so when decisions are being made on prioritizing what are often limited resources. Think A, B, C of everything—customer promise, *inventory policy*, replenishment strategies, distribution strategies. It even has been applied and found true in how much value sales representatives deliver. The Integrated Tactical Planning process is meant to operate at a more detailed level, which means even more data points. How do we make sense of more data points? We prioritize what is more important so we can focus.

However, management of this is sometime seen as counterintuitive. For example, when it is applied to inventory policy, the intuitive approach is, "My biggest and most important SKUs need to have more inventory cover to protect our most important customers' requirements." This is actually the opposite thinking to what is required. The strategy needs to be set to cover the noise from the C items to free time to focus on the A items. The problem is that there are so many C items that they create far more noise, attract the most attention, but add little value. If something creates a lot of noise, we as humans tend to respond, regardless of the value in doing so.

In the case of C items, we need strategies to take away the noise, so in fact, we may decide to hold proportionately more safety stock for Cs to free time to focus deliberately on our star items. The simple math behind this is that if we raise inventory by 20% for all C items, that is 20% on 5% of the volume and value, which translates to only a 1% increase overall. If we raise safety stock by 20% on all A items, that is 20% of 80%, which translates to a 16% increase overall.

We'll discuss more on this in Chapter 5, but the important point with respect to the Integrated Tactical Planning process is to do the math and then agree on what behaviors we'd like from people in the business when managing SKUs, customers, and suppliers. Contrary to conventional wisdom, modern business thinking is that you'll get a better return for your investment by focusing on the big things that are going well than trying to continually fix the annoying fringe elements.

This discussion nicely leads on to the standard customer promise, which in most businesses completely ignores the Pareto principle.

Prioritizing the Customer Promise in Which All Customers and Products Are Not Equal

In most organizations, the customer promising logic is simple, that is, first in, first served; and when we run out of stock, we'll let everyone know to stop selling and stop placing orders.

Yet if you walk into the customer service department, they can usually tell you who the best customers are and how they jump through hoops to make sure they get what they want. Similarly, if you ask supply chain, they would have a view of the same thing, maybe based on how many special requirements the customer has. If you then asked sales, they would have a third view, based on where they think they may gain extra sales or where they are in the contract negotiations. That's when we would usually ask if the company has agreed across the functions to a company-wide *ABC classification* of products and whether they have set their priorities accordingly. This is usually the point of realization that priorities are functionally based, and not coordinated to serve the business as a whole.

Figure 2.6 is an example of how companies could get alignment, not only on the math but also on defining the behavioral expectations from the analysis. Often when we ask companies whether they do a Pareto assessment on SKUs, someone in supply chain or operations will reply in the affirmative. The next question is to ask what we do with that analysis, which is usually greeted with silence or "we sent it around to everyone but never got a response." The killer question is to ask what happened the next time there was a problem, and the answer usually is that they reverted to type with every person defending his or her own version of the truth.

	A SKUs	B SKUs	C SKUs
A Customers	We will maintain ... 98% DIFOT??	We will ... ??	We will ... ??
B Customers	We will ... ??	We will ... ??	We will ... ??
C Customers	We will ... ??	We will ... ??	We will ... ??

FIGURE 2.6 Customer Promise

Source: Oliver Wight. Copyright Oliver Wight International, Inc. Used with permission.

The inputs required are an ABC analysis of SKUs by volume, revenue, and profit and the same for customers/channels/segments. This often also uncovers vulnerabilities, such as with one client who undertook an ABC assessment and found that their number one volume item, to their number one customer, was in fact, not making much money. The important outcome is not the analysis itself; it is defining what behavioral expectations are for each of the boxes in Figure 2.6.

The AAs and CCs are usually straightforward to define. The company will do whatever it takes to protect the AA business, and the CC might need different supply strategies or longer commitment times. By way of illustration, a large steel manufacturer revised their customer ordering policy for minor specialty steel parts ordered by metal fabrication companies. They said that if the parts are C items for a C customer, they will still offer them in their portfolio, but they will make them only twice a year. If the forecast is right and the order is placed on time, then the customer should expect to have their order fulfilled, but if not, the customer can wait for the next campaign production, which could be up to 6 months away.

The hard part is what do you do with the AB, AC, BA, and other less obvious classifications. It is usually a tough job to get all stakeholders aligned, but it must be done; otherwise, the company will end up doing it informally and without proper coordination or consideration. Once it is done in an unconstrained environment, it then needs to be done again for when there might be an ongoing supply constraint.

Once drafted, agreed to, and communicated, the organization then has something to bring to life within Integrated Tactical Planning. The intent of the Integrated Tactical Planning process is to rebalance plans or escalate otherwise, and to work effectively it should empower people to make decisions at the lowest possible level and get on with execution, avoiding escalating unless absolutely necessary.

This is an appropriate segue to what do we do if we have to escalate.

Effective Escalation Criteria and Communication

As mentioned in the previous section, the role of the Integrated Tactical Planning process is to rebalance tactical plans back to the plans as signed off in the last Integrated Business Planning cycle, and most of the time if plans are valid and unbiased that team should be capable of doing that without intervention. If the plans can't be rebalanced, people need to know who the decision authorities are, and to whom to escalate.

Figure 2.7 is a simple example of three escalation points and a description of the type of change, the tolerances that may be applied, and who would sign off the change in plans.

	Type of Change	Tolerances	Authorization
Inside the Planning Time Fence	Minor changes in demand or supply	Less than $?? Within key measure tolerances	Supply Planner Demand Manager Line Supervisor
	Moderate change, that may cost money or cut into safety or affect an A customer	Within +/-$?? Key measures may be affected.	Sales Director Finance Director Supply Chain Director
	Major change, that will cost significant money or have a big impact on customer service	Greater than $?? Considerable impact on customer service and financial projections	CEO

FIGURE 2.7 Example Escalation Criteria

Source: Oliver Wight. Copyright Oliver Wight International, Inc. Used with permission.

Often these criteria are applied only to changes in the demand plan and/or sales orders, but it should be applied to any change to the product, demand, and supply plans inside the PTF. The reason is that there needs to be a level of formality and documentation to facilitate analysis of the root causes and the potential for applying the learning to reduce the number of changes over time.

The logic applies for the whole PTF, but there should be even tighter controls and tolerances applied when the change affects the next couple of weeks because the disruption and cost is likely to be higher. This time fence will be discussed in more detail in the demand and supply sections, but suffice it to say now that there should only be emergency changes in the very short term.

The simple change criteria we often see in companies are usually just value based with a certain monetary amount triggering escalations. However, it is recommended that the impact on key metrics and the impact on strategies on managing normal cause variation in demand and supply plans also be included. For example, if the change is going to cause the customer delivery metric to drop below 98%, and/or 50% of safety stock is going to be consumed, then that might trigger the escalation process.

Key metrics usually have an agreed tolerance anyway; for example, the master supply plan metric often is defined as finished goods ready to be shipped on the due date plus or minus 5% on volume. As long as the metric is still going to be delivered this month within the agreed tolerance, the change is approved by individuals tasked with maintaining valid plans.

They would also be expected to communicate and agree to these changes with all who are affected.

Remember, the intent is to empower people as close to the action as possible to make decisions. The process needs to be able to respond quickly, especially when the company is dealing with a high number of customer or production orders each day and when lead times are very short.

Use of Demonstrated Capability in Building Realistic Plans

Building realistic plans is at the heart of excellent execution and demonstrated capability is what underpins excellence in execution. Most supply organizations understand this well, and although we'll expand on this further in Chapter 5, it is a vital concept for the organization as a whole to understand, practice, and use as a guide to the thinking behind the Integrated Tactical Planning process.

Let's start with the supply example depicted in Figure 2.8. A fundamental predictor of a valid plan is to analyze and use previous performance as a baseline. Unless something has changed, future performance can't be any different than your past performance. We often hear, however, statements such as, "The team is committed to being more focused," or "All those one-off incidents that slowed us up last time; they will not happen again." Or, worst of all, "It's been committed to in *budget* and we therefore have no choice but to assume we're going to be able to do it." This is usually accompanied by the words "we hope," but we all know hope is not a strategy, and

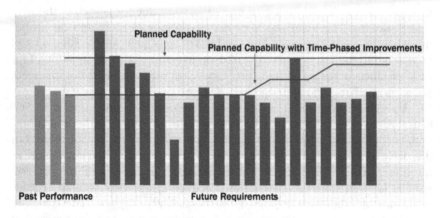

FIGURE 2.8 Demonstrated Capability

Source: Oliver Wight. Copyright Oliver Wight International, Inc. Used with permission.

similarly doing the same thing over and over again and expecting a different outcome is a sign of insanity.

Figure 2.8 is a real client example. The green bars are 3 weeks of history, the blue bars are future requirements, and the red lines are the assessed capability. The top red line was the company's initial assessment of capability and, as can be seen, there is an issue only with the current week, but plenty of spare capability to catch up later, right? The warning sign, however, is the overloaded current week, which indicates that there might be what we call a *bow wave*, which is when anything that you failed to make this week gets pushed forward into next week because the organization thinks it has the capability to catch up, but in reality is it just getting further and further behind or pushing requirements out indefinitely? On deeper investigation with this company, people agreed that this was the case and had been that way for months.

Then the real question "How do you calculate your capability?" was answered. This turned out to be an annual process as part of the *business budget*, with no routine way of checking the validity in between. Even then the number that had been calculated was subjected to 5% to 10% uplift to match what was needed to close the gap to budget and balance the numbers.

When the site deployed a demonstrated capacity planning process, the problem appeared even worse (the lower red line), but at least it was real and they could start proactively doing something about it, as opposed to evoking the hope strategy.

Demonstrated capability does not just apply to production capacity. Another example is in the new product space where the company had 20 new products to launch in a year and most were due for launch in the next 3 to 6 months. The team was very nervous about the plan and on further investigation we uncovered a few key facts that could have alleviated a lot of heartache. In the last 3 years they had, on average, managed to launch four new products a year, and their processes and resources had not changed. So, without changing anything, their *demonstrated performance* was four.

A similar example can be applied to the demand generation area. Statistical forecasting packages work from sales history to compute projections, and, yes, there are a lot of sophisticated algorithms in the background, but the basic premise is that the trends found in history will be replicated in the future. This is demonstrated performance. The behavioral expectation is what is often called *anchoring* in that even in the most volatile of sales environments, the starting point is the statistical projection. The dialogue then becomes centered on what is going to be different in the future that would cause a departure of the new forecast from the statistical projections.

The counterargument we often hear is that if we don't give people stretch goals, then they will not try to achieve any more than the bare minimum, but our experience, and the science on human motivation for that matter, is different. Take the metaphor that is often cited: "If you shoot for the moon, you might at least be able summit Everest." This is known as a *cognitive bias/logical fallacy*—it sounds logical, but it is totally wrong. Logic it out in practical terms. Each goal will need a completely different set of plans, resources, and specific equipment to get to the moon, as opposed to summitting Everest. Similarly, if we set ourselves up for the stretch but only get a bit of it, we not only demotivate people but also we will have wasted the required resources.

Managing Uncertainty Through Scenario Planning

As the often-used quote goes, "If I could predict the future accurately, I wouldn't be doing this job—I'd be at the races every Wednesday betting on the horses and working the stock market in my spare time." Unfortunately, we can't predict the future with 100% accuracy, and organizations need to accept that there are going to be errors in plans. Although excellence is about minimizing errors, there is always going to be uncertainty about planning for the future.

When we set up the Integrated Tactical Planning process and its supporting metrics, we build around this error with tolerances and targets based on how close our processes and plans can deliver that 100% accuracy. These then form the basis for building the safety net to support that error. Safety stock is one form of safety, but there are others, such as *lead-time offset* and safety time. This is all to protect against normal cause variation, which we mentioned previously.

There are, however, circumstances that go beyond normal cause variation that require a deeper level of thought and analysis, which is where scenario planning comes in. A rule of thumb for doing scenarios is when the potential uncertainty exceeds our ability to cost-effectively plan for it. One good example is launching a new product, especially if it is new to the company, or new to the world, and there are no historical reference points to guide forecasts.

Logically, you could say that from an Integrated Tactical Planning process perspective, many of these simulations would have been done in the planning phase, outside the PTF, and hence there will only be a need to execute the contingency plans that were generated to support the simulation. In practice, however, as the aggregate Integrated Business Planning process moves closer to today, there is a deeper level of granularity in plans, and the *time zones* usually go from months outside the PTF, to weeks, and then to days. When you enter into the lower level of granularity you often find that there is more, or a different level of uncertainty uncovered, than first anticipated, which needs further evaluation and preparation.

Simulation capability becomes all the more important to be able to assess various scenarios before making commitments. Mostly the planning system can handle the changes. For example, a customer orders 10% more than usual. The order can be seen consuming inventory, and an impact on the consumption of safety stock can be done quite simply. Similarly, when *available-to-promise* capability is used, it is a simulation tool that looks out to the future production or supply plans and tests a promise against that future supply.

However, that 10% increase in one customer's order might be the first sign of a bigger change brewing. There could be a range of reasons, such as a competitor has had a quality-hold issue, or put up prices unexpectedly, or a raw ingredient is in short supply. What the Integrated Tactical Planning quorum wants to be able to do is adjust the plans and test the impact beforehand.

Aside from some of the great tools that can do this in real time, as Figure 2.9 suggests, consideration needs to be given to the process that sits in behind it, as we'll explore further in the following sections.

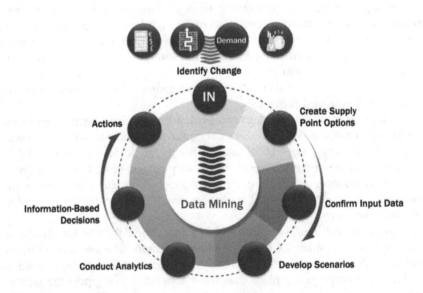

FIGURE 2.9 Scenario Planning

Source: Oliver Wight. Copyright Oliver Wight International, Inc. Used with permission.

IDENTIFY THE CHANGE   This sounds simple, but without being in control in the first place, changes are just a way of life in many companies. The assumption is that minor changes can and will occur and most people just accept them as part of the normal cause variation that their processes are set up to deal with. The key is to know when a change is significant enough or when a group of changes are indicating something bigger is occurring. For practical reasons, though, you simulate every possibility all the time. The recommendation is that the tools are set up beforehand based on likely parameters that could be affected.

For those who have run various scenarios in spreadsheets, you'll know that to set one up from scratch can be a labor of love, and even if it is already set up, it can take several hours to reconfigure for the new parameters. I asked a planner from a company that sells eggs if they run scenarios inside their Integrated Tactical Planning horizon and she said that they did it often. Eggs vary in size and quality through the age of the hen and time of year and can affect the price the customer is willing to pay. So, the planners are constantly trying to level their flocks to optimize availability *and* price. When she was asked how long it took to update the spreadsheet with the latest parameters, she said at least half a day. In this age of technology, that is about 3.75 hours too long!

DEFINE THE VARIABLES   I mentioned technology, and it is true that there are wonderful tools available today. However, none of them yet can do the thinking for you. You need to do the background work and, as with the egg example, their primary drivers were size of the flock, quality of the egg, and price, but the issue was that those parameters varied significantly from one flock site to another. In other industries it could be lead times, service levels, costs, inventory levels, and customer order quantities, to name just a few. As Dell did in their early days, cash-to-cash cycle time drove dramatic changes (for the time) in supply chain structure, to the point that Dell had achieved a negative cash-to-cash cycle time, which meant they were being paid by the customer well before paying their suppliers.

The point is to understand the key drivers for your business and set up models to be ready.

CONFIRM INPUT DATA   If the simulation environment has been set up well, then the information comes straight out of the planning system, which in turn means that the data in the planning system need to be accurate. In the previous example of planning for egg availability, she said it took her half a day to create the scenarios, but then another half a day to correct errors, chase down strange numbers, and fix broken links. The lesson? No matter how sophisticated the software, maintaining data integrity is absolutely fundamental.

In a gross example of how this might escalate out of control, one of our clients was thinking of upgrading their ERP system and, as part of the due diligence, surveyed how many data holding and planning spreadsheets were in the business. This business had 1,000 employees and they found 80,000 spreadsheets and 8,000 were still active. How do you control this amount of uncontrolled data? The answer: you don't!

DEVELOP THE SCENARIOS AND ANALYTICS   If the modeling environment has been set up appropriately, the data integrity is accurate and trusted, source data are controlled out of an enterprise system, then the scenarios should be a matter of just adjusting key parameters—but which parameters?

This is where a demand planner got into a bit of trouble. Up until recently, she was only asked for three scenarios—upside, downside, and realistic. As her spreadsheet skills improved, she was asked for variations within each of those scenarios, and within a short space of time, the usual three scenarios had mushroomed to 27 and still were increasing. What got her in trouble was that she could keep the underlying parameters in her head with three variations, but with 27 she couldn't remember each scenario's underlying *assumptions*.

The lesson? Document the variables and assumption changes and add only detail and complexity where needed and where it can be kept under control.

TAKE ACTION   This is going to sound like a no-brainer but it must be said. Once the analytics have been done, it must be supported by action plans. The question that must be answered is, "If that scenario eventuates, what are we going to do?" This means not only risk mitigation and contingency plans but also plans to leverage opportunities should they arise. Occasionally we see simulations done, but then no one considers actions to put in place or trigger points to implement the simulation. That is missing a huge opportunity to get ahead of the competitors.

RECOGNIZE CHANGE MANAGEMENT AS AN EVERYDAY MANAGEMENT PRACTICE Change management gets talked about all the time, and most of the organizations we work with have an extensive change management process, templates, and assistance, but they often fail to use them effectively. Why? Usually it is seen as only for the big projects, and everything else is just normal day-to-day management. We have a different view; change management *is* what management does, so the tool sets need to be a routine part of a manager's daily role.

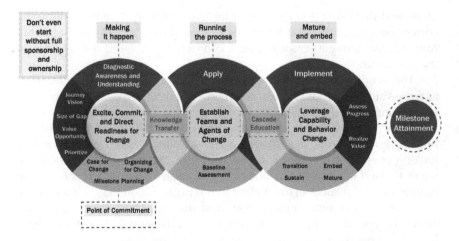

FIGURE 2.10 Change Management

Source: Oliver Wight. Copyright Oliver Wight International, Inc. Used with permission.

The Integrated Tactical Planning process is no different. To make the change requires a proven methodology for not only making the change but also making the change stick.

Figure 2.10 shows the change journey, and the important point of this is that for change to stick, every element needs to be addressed—you can't shortcut any of it. The first and most vital point is that to get the change underway, full executive team sponsorship and ownership is a must. If you don't have this, then it's like trying to push water uphill.

MAKE IT HAPPEN To get that executive team buy-in, we need to make sure there is excitement for the possibilities that leads to commitment and readiness for the change. This can be in the form of creating the vision of the future that entices them, or alternatively, in some cases, by highlighting the burning platform on which they're standing and encouraging them to jump off to safety. Both involve the assessment of the gap between current practices and what excellence looks like—it just depends on which factor is likely to motivate them more.

It is then important to translate that back to the business with a journey-visioning session to describe what it is going to look like for the business and how we want people to behave—most importantly starting with the executive team. Many leaders do not appreciate that the change starts with them, and that often it is their behavior that needs to change to allow the correct decision rights and processes to exist throughout the organization. After all, like any gift, empowerment can only be received if it is given in the first instance.

The scoping process needs to assess the size of the gaps identified and the value that could be realized in closing those gaps to determine the sequencing and priorities. In one rapidly growing dairy company, there was a window, about 150 feet long, in the offices that looked over the primary finished goods warehouse. When we asked, "What's with the long window looking over the warehouse?" the answer was, "So everyone knows when we're making too much and not selling enough." The CEO and founding partner of the business made it clear to the organization that "We are going to become a planning organization, and inventory will never again rise above the bottom of the window." The point of the story is that visions don't have to be out there but can be practical and compelling.

This one sentence captured the vision and size of the gap because they were not a planning organization at the time. The value (the cost of off-site inventory storage and managing short-dated and obsolescent inventory) was easily calculated and was in the millions of dollars. Think of the dynamics of a dairy business. Milk comes in everyday regardless of whether the company is ready for it or has demand. It needs to be converted into something within 36 hours, and that product also has a relatively short shelf life. Most sales are to a commodity environment, which means the price can move dramatically within weeks. Some would argue that you can't plan for an environment like that, but we see it as fertile ground for an Integrated Tactical Planning process.

The final two important elements of the case for change are to build it so people understand WIIFM (what's in it for me) individually, for their functions, and for the business, and allocate appropriate resources to stack the cards for success.

RUN THE PROCESS   If in the first stage of making it happen, as mentioned, the critical element is executive team sponsorship and ownership, then in this next phase, knowledge transfer is vital. You can't expect people to do things for you unless you show them what is expected and how it is to be done. This is when agents of change are being developed, and processes are being piloted. If it is planned well, a robust Integrated Tactical Planning process can be matured in as little as 12 weeks.

In the dairy company mentioned previously, their plan was 4 weeks piloting, 4 weeks rolling out, and 4 weeks refining and fine-tuning. At the end of the 12 weeks we checked in on the gaps to see what an excellent process looks like and then saw them continue to systematically improve thereafter. Will it be operating at the 95% performance level that we have mentioned previously? Probably not, but will it be showing benefits that make the business sit up and see the potential that it offers? Almost definitely.

MATURE AND EMBED   This third stage is all about sustainability. The simple but powerful definition of *sustain* is that when key people move on from the process or business, the Integrated Tactical Planning process will not only continue to exist but also will have enough momentum to continue its evolution and improvement.

The key elements for sustainability are education, procedures, and performance management. Education needs to be continuous, starting when a person joins the company or enters a role, and then at regular intervals to both act as a reminder as well as kicking off another wave of improvement. The latest ways of working are reflected in the policies and procedures, and these are actively adhered to and used as a reference source. The performance management process recognizes people's roles in the process and appraises their performance accordingly.

KNOW THAT IT IS NEVER SMOOTH SAILING   As one bright and energetic HR manager once said, "Everyone loves a change—holiday, night out, receiving gifts—but no one likes to be changed!" A fundamental truth is that we are all individuals, and we go through the change loop (see Figure 2.11) at different speeds and interpret things differently. Neither is right or wrong. There have been more than 130 human biases identified that can distort people's perception, engagement, and commitment to change, and as any transformation manager will testify, every change program will see all of them at one stage or another.

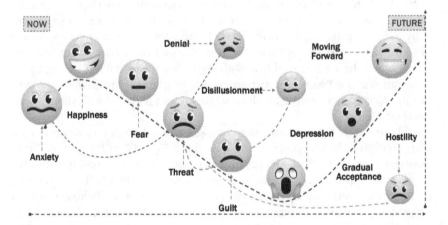

FIGURE 2.11 Change Can Be an Emotional Rollercoaster

Source: **Oliver Wight. Copyright Oliver Wight International, Inc. Used with permission.**

One thing is certain, if people are excluded, they will make the change even harder. Some people, however, only need to see the vision of the future and then will jump in with both feet. They are the people we want on the core team to help drive change. Others will nervously dip their toe in the water; some will stand on the side waiting to see what happens to those who went before them; then there are those who will dig their heels in. It is important that individuals are recognized for where they are on this change loop. If management behavior is aligned with them, it is more likely to get positive results.

Here are the six keys to managing the breadth of people and their responses:

- Create a network map of the sponsors, reinforcing sponsors, influencers, change agents, solution builders, and resisters.
- Develop the key messages for each category and evolution of the deployment.
- Tap into the strengths and capabilities of the willing.
- Keep the deployment safe until people understand the impact and what is required of them, which makes piloting, applying the learning, and deliberately planning the rollout vital.
- Publish the wins, all the wins, all of the time.
- Be proactive in identifying and managing the resisters ahead of time.

Summary and Key Change Requirements

In this section we have covered the key elements of making the Integrated Tactical Planning process work. Time fences and the rules for change are mission critical to communicate that the cost of change increases exponentially the closer the change is to today. There needs to be a cross-functional quorum of people to trap and manage changes on a daily/weekly basis. Focus has to be on the vital few with strategies for managing the rest, and although we need to set escalation criteria in plan for approving changes, the intent is to get people as close to the action as possible making decisions on change.

There needs to be commitment to a plan based on demonstrated capability that puts the customer promise as the raison d'être for why we're in business first, as well as recognizing the need to model multiple futures to plan for uncertainty. Finally, managing change needs to be something that is done every day by managers and is critical if there is going to be a large change such as designing and deploying an Integrated Tactical Planning process.

In the next few chapters we're going to dive into a little more detail to add context to the overview concepts and will then surface toward the end of the book with what a process might look like and what the agenda of the weekly meeting might look like for your business.

PEOPLE AND BEHAVIOR CHANGES
- A quorum of roles needs to be defined to own core plans.
- Adherence to time fences is critical.
- The first 3 months of the Integrated Business Planning process plans are the guiding set of plans for the Integrated Tactical Planning process.
- Not all customers and SKUs are equal.

PROCESS CHANGES
- Time fences need to be defined for critical decision points.
- Escalation criteria definitions are critical for running the business by exception.
- Use the Pareto principle to focus on the vital few customers and SKUs.
- Demonstrated capability underlies all plans.
- Taking a change-management approach is an imperative.

TECHNOLOGY CHANGES
- Use the system for assessing the vital few.
- Use the planning modules in the system, not spreadsheets, for planning and data holding.
- Simulation capability is essential for modeling and assessing multiple futures.
- Set up the time fences in the system.

CHAPTER 3

Delivering the Value

Executing the Product Plan

In this chapter we are going to dive a little deeper into the elements needed to successfully execute the product plan within Integrated Tactical Planning. We will cover the three broad areas of portfolio management, project management, and resource management, but before we start we need to align on a few definitions to be clear about what we mean by *product, new,* and *portfolio.*

Definition of Product and Portfolio

When we refer to *product* we mean *products and services.* Many physical goods companies have services that they provide for their physical product, without which the physical product may be less attractive or practical. For example, if you bought a new car and there was no specialist servicing provided, you're unlikely to be very happy. Similarly, service providers, such as banks, don't sell physical goods, but they usually have to consider some physical products, such as brochures and pamphlets to support their services. So, to Oliver Wight, the term *product* spans both physical and nonphysical products.

The term *portfolio* means all the activities that concern individuals and the suite of products in their life cycle, such as deciding which products and services you will offer the market through to the addition of new products, the deletion or phaseout of old products, and modifications to individual products and services.

Defining the Elements of Product and Portfolio

It is important for a company to define what is managed under the product portfolio remit and hence what will be managed through to execution by the Integrated Tactical Planning process. A basic way to look at it is that if a product's SKU number changes, then that new SKU should be included in the product portfolio plan because there will be a series of tasks required to ensure that the change is achieved. So, what constitutes a SKU number change? The primary definition is that if a SKU, or item for that matter, differs in form, fit, or function, it should have a new number. If that is not the default process in your company, then it may be causing some confusion.

In most companies the *new* definitions can be defined (or refined) from the list in Figure 3.1.

Depending on the company's strategy, there are often only a few new-to-the-world and/or new-to-the-company products at any one time but a high number of additions to product lines—changes, improvements, and rationalization; cost reductions; and repositioning projects—going on at the same time. The reason we need to define more precisely and categorize what is new is that they vary in terms of cost, risk, and consumption of resources. New-to-the-world products often have more uncertainty, need much more investment, and require more technical resources than some of the other categories. If successful, however, the rewards should also be correspondingly higher.

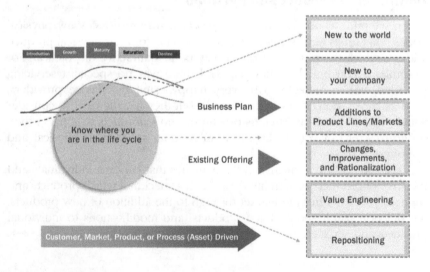

FIGURE 3.1 What Is "New" to the Business?

Source: Oliver Wight. Copyright Oliver Wight International, Inc. Used with permission.

Similar to the Pareto principle, if not appropriately managed, the small number of high-reward projects can get overshadowed by the many smaller-return projects. What we need to be aware of is the overall resource *load* to complete each project on time and what mechanisms can be put in place to spend time on the big projects, while not losing track of the small-return ones. This is why it is so important to have the role of product project manager and for the portfolio plans to be represented in the Integrated Tactical Planning process.

There are, however, exceptions. For example, an *engineer to order (ETO)* supply strategy means that every order would be unique and have a separate product number. This is the business's go-to-market strategy and hence would be managed in a business-as-usual (BAU) process. By way of example, one of our clients who make excavators has a standard 1-meter-wide bucket that is used to dig trenches, but a customer ordered a 900 mm bucket. The question is, "Should that be considered part of the portfolio management of all SKUs, or is it a BAU process?" In this case the company chose to define it as a BAU ETO process because for all intents and purposes, it was exactly the same specifications and production process as the standard bucket—it was just slightly narrower. An ETO environment, such as this example, should also be supported by an order validation process to check on design, capacity, material, and price, and then promise the order against the consumption of the capacity in the master supply plan, which we'll talk more about in Chapter 5. Incidentally, in this example, the difference in how much earth is moved when digging a 10 km trench is enormous, and therefore the 900 mm bucket is going to save the customer a lot of labor and time.

In this same example, if there were an opportunity to use a stronger or lighter material in the bucket, which has never been produced before, then this project would be more effectively defined as new and managed through the *product portfolio management* process as a change of design.

Another example to ponder is from a global food company, which has a big new customer in a part of the world they have never supplied before, but the requirement is for a standard product from their existing portfolio. Where does that fit? Usually it would be managed through the sales and marketing team's BAU demand and customer management processes, but in certain circumstances, it might be such a radical change to the supply chain, regulatory rules, and consumption of raw materials that it would be better managed through the product portfolio disciplines. This is an example of repositioning of a product within a new market (as noted in Figure 3.1).

As you can see, defining what is new for the company is critical to not only the Integrated Tactical Planning process but also to the business's overall strategic approach.

Scope of Product and Portfolio Process

A way to depict the levels of responsibility and time frames is via the graphic in Figure 3.2

At a strategic level and horizon, which is usually at least 3 to 5 years, there are road maps for marketing, technology, supply chain, demand, and other supporting functions and elements. As the time horizon comes into today, the top-down road maps meet the bottom-up ideas and market conditions and start filling the *funnel* of the *stage-and-gate process*. At about Stage 2 (creating the business case), the business should be getting closer to execution, which is where this overlaps into the Integrated Tactical Planning process. Although it is still a funnel, and not all ideas will get through to launch, the management of activities that need to go into assessing the go/no-go decision at each gate thereafter could affect the Integrated Tactical Planning process horizon.

The product portfolio plan is often seen as a longer-range plan, and so it should be. There is a time, however, when the product portfolio plan moves into execution, and often that is left to the project teams to be independently pulling the strings to make the project happen on time. In an Integrated Tactical Planning environment, the product portfolio plans are managed alongside the demand, supply, and customer plans, and the product project manager is part of the quorum to represent and make sure those product plans stay on track inside the planning time fence.

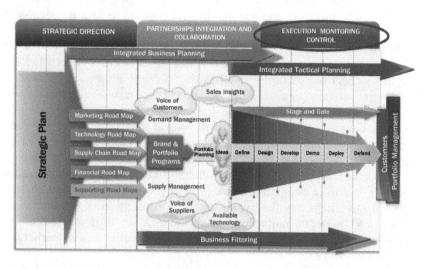

FIGURE 3.2 Product Control and Execution

Source: Oliver Wight. Copyright Oliver Wight International, Inc. Used with permission.

Coming back to that key term *portfolio,* it is important to stress again that it is more than just about new product launch plans, and although new products are a significant part of the product portfolio planning, other plans that need to be considered are those relating to minor product changes, managing SKU deletions, making sure trials go to plan, and effectively managing the prelaunch inventory and sample plans.

Integrated Tactical Planning Horizon

Once the definitions of *product, portfolio,* and *new* are clear, the area of the Integrated Planning model that needs to be considered is depicted in Figure 3.3. It lives in the below-the-line detailed area and across the product, demand, and supply planning and execution disciplines.

Although the horizon of the Integrated Tactical Planning process is typically about 13 weeks, in the product area it is frequently extended for specific categories mentioned in Figure 3.1. This should be a special

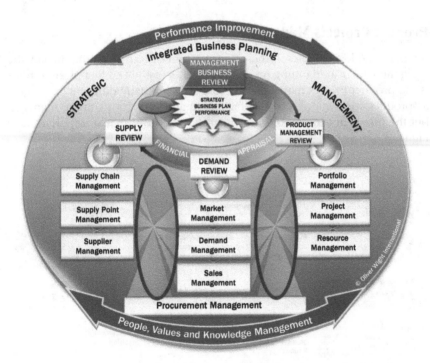

FIGURE 3.3 Below-the-Line Product Control Using Demand and Supply Planning

Source: Oliver Wight. Copyright Oliver Wight International, Inc. Used with permission.

horizon for new-to-the-world and new-to the-business projects to ensure a level of focus and visibility as those projects move toward the critical stage of launch. To make sure management resist the temptation to crash new products into the schedule, it is recommended that a must-meet criterion at the last gate before launch reads something like, "Launch date will not be before . . . [specified time period]." The reason is that even though everything is a go for launch, there will be a number of actions still to be done, and if the business rushes that final set of actions, things are likely to be skipped over or forgotten.

From a capacity perspective, this should have been assessed in the Integrated Business Planning process many months prior hitting the go button, and indeed, if significant new capacity is needed, it might have been flagged several years prior. It is critical that the resource requirements are considered in more detail inside the launch window as well as supporting contingencies for the what-if questions, such as, "What if the runs rates are slower than the trials indicated?" The important part of this is that in the replanning process, the product portfolio plan is honored alongside all other plans.

Product Projects Manager

As mentioned in Chapter 2, there is a quorum of four roles that makes the Integrated Tactical Planning process work effectively. The first of these roles is the product project manager. The role goes by many different titles, such as product coordinator, product facilitator, and product planning manager, but the title is not important; it is what the role does that is important (see Figure 3.4).

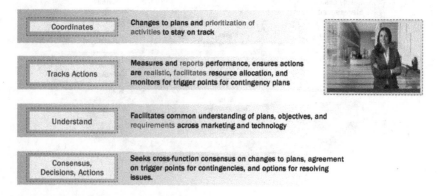

FIGURE 3.4 Product Planning Manager Role

Source: Oliver Wight. Copyright Oliver Wight International, Inc. Used with permission.

Depending on the size of the organization, this could be the one role or many roles. In smaller organizations, the role may span facilitation of the *product management review* of the Integrated Business Planning process, and in larger organizations it could be part of a product portfolio management team.

Whatever way the organization is structured, the intent of this role is to ensure the execution part of the product plan stays on track, and if there are changes, they are effectively coordinated in a cross-function environment through the Integrated Tactical Planning process.

While the product planning manager is working to optimize and re-optimize the product plan over the mid- to long-term horizon through the Integrated Business Planning process, for the Integrated Tactical Planning process, the product project manager takes the monthly product portfolio plan out to the planning time fence and breaks it down into a weekly buckets, and even into daily buckets, as the plan gets closer to execution. This role coordinates changes to the overall plan, which arise during the week, and analyzes the impact of those changes over the Integrated Tactical Planning horizon. Working in collaboration with product project teams, customer service, the *demand execution* manager, and the master supply scheduler, the product projects manager develops potential solutions and facilitates consensus on the way forward. If an effective way forward can't be found without significant cost or impact on an area of the business, the person would also manage the escalation for authorization.

This role also entails the collation and assessment of changes to the underpinning assumptions, which have caused the change to plan. Assumptions are an important part of any Integrated Business Planning process, including the product management review, and they are meant to describe the thinking behind the plan in such a way they can be quantified and measured for accuracy. The role also tracks and measures completion of actions to ensure plans remain valid, resources are adequate, and that the person is scanning the environment for trigger points to enact the contingencies should anticipated upside-downside conditions occur. Measuring actions completed and the number of changes also provides a rich source of information and insights to fold back into planning to improve certainty in execution of future projects.

The manager would also be responsible for, or part of, a team doing the analysis and modeling of the current portfolio of products, understanding the performance of the plan, tracking funnel movements, checking on the status of actions and improvement plans, and engaging in scenario and *contingency planning*. The manager would be acting as the conduit for a common understanding of the plan and aligning different perspectives to ensure decisions get made and product-related actions get completed on time.

Product Life Cycle

As we keep saying, this is not just launching new products. There are a number of product portfolio–related activities that also need to be managed. To add to the previous discussion about defining what is new, there are other activities to include, such as the phasing out of products identified for deletion. This is also an area that can cause contention. Sales and marketing will want to hold onto anything that is adding to their revenue and margin, supply chain and operations will want to remove the disproportionate amount of noise that small-volume products cause, and finance will want to avoid obsolescence of the slow-moving items. It's not surprising then, that many of our clients start off with large numbers of products we refer to as "the dead and the dying" in their portfolio, which nobody will take the responsibility to put out of their misery.

There are a number of good business reasons for products to be deleted, such as being delisted by the trade, a new product cannibalizing an existing product, or it has reached the criteria set for end of life. Figure 3.5 depicts a typical product life cycle, where sales are represented by the red line, profit is represented by the gray line, and cash generated is represented by the dotted red line, as the product transitions through introduction, growth, maturity, saturation, and decline.

Companies tend not to do *product life cycle management and assessment* well, but as discussed in Chapter 2, true profitability of the C items is usually marginal at best and is often negative.

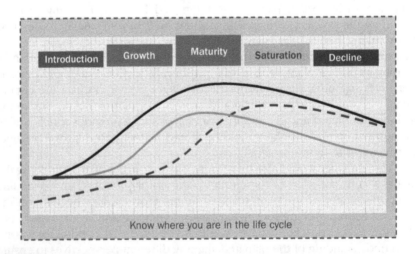

FIGURE 3.5 Product Life Cycle Curve

Source: Oliver Wight. Copyright Oliver Wight International, Inc. Used with permission.

Although the management of the product life cycle is part of the Integrated Business Planning process, the execution of the plan rests with Integrated Tactical Planning. The objective is to understand where each product fits in its life cycle inside the Integrated Tactical Planning time fence and therefore where the focus should be for the product control process.

Bringing this all together shows that excellence in product control is multifaceted and may result in a workload that comes in waves during the year. Most grocery outlets, for example, have two windows a year for new-product negotiations, seasonal products have a once-a-year window, and seasonal raw materials, similarly, may only have a small window to source and use appropriate raw ingredients.

We will discuss inventory policy in more detail in Chapter 5, but for us at Oliver Wight, inventory policy is a much underrated, and sometimes maligned, set of activities and policies. If we had our way, we would call it something like, "the agreement to the cost of the supply strategy to meet our customer service requirements, maintain competitiveness, cover lead times, cover against uncertainty, manage lot sizing, and keep the product portfolio manageable and profitable." Ha-ha! That is a mouthful but describes what we'd expect to see in an inventory policy, and we'd be delighted if any of our readers can come up with something more succinct.

However, one of the elements of the inventory policy should be the D-for-delete section, supported by a set of objective criteria for flagging products for deletion from the portfolio. The following are starting points for defining the criteria:

- Forecast volume is below XX units per month.
- Gross margin is below YY%.
- It is not strategic or a growing new product.
- It is not part of a range.
- It is not a companion sale for an A item.

If all the criteria are met, the way we like to phrase it, is that the item *will be deleted,* unless justification is made to keep it. All too often the justification is the other way around; there is a requirement for someone to justify deleting them. This just drives the wrong behavior in that it is easier to do nothing than work up the justification.

Integration with Demand-Supply Tactical Execution

Too often the right information is not available when required, and the process turns into one that rewards the person who shouts loudest. As depicted in Figure 3.6, there are time horizons, gate approvals, and stakeholders

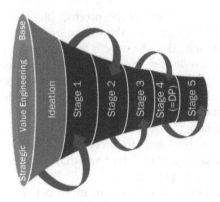

FIGURE 3.6 Demand-Supply Information Required for Tactical Execution

Source: Oliver Wight. Copyright Oliver Wight International, Inc. Used with permission.

involved that need certain information at certain times, and that information should become increasingly more granular as the launch dates get closer to today.

The intent of a stage-and-gate process is to eliminate those projects that don't meet the company's definition of success as defined in the gate criteria. Hence the depiction in Figure 3.6 is a funnel. The other intent is to make sure investment in projects occurs in a staged manner; for example, while a project is in ideation, it is not likely a company would start building a multimillion-dollar production facility site, until at least the business plan is approved.

There are different terms that companies use for each stage and each gate, but to be able to contextualize this section, the following is a brief overview of what Oliver Wight call the Six Ds of a stage-and-gate process, which typically follows the ideation stage:

1. Define—investigate the potential.
2. Design—build the business case and estimate annual sales.
3. Develop—develop the idea further, prototype, and create a fuzzy forecast.
4. Demonstrate—test and validate, firm the forecast in the demand plan, and finalize planning parameters and *master data.*
5. Deploy—produce and launch.
6. Defend—*postlaunch review* and manage the product life cycle.

However, most of the gate requirements for a stage-and-gate process are determined by people with a technical background, and so the needs of the wider organization are often overlooked. Here are some of the areas that we have seen companies trip themselves up with:

- Does the organization understand how long it takes to set up a new item and bills of material in the system?
- Can the system manage ghost SKUs, which are used to plan products in their fuzzy stage before the bills of material and financials are finalized?
- Who will manage these ghost SKUs?
- When will a monthly time-phased forecast be needed?
- When will trials be scheduled and who will be responsible?
- How will the inventory build be managed prelaunch, and who is going to do it?
- How and when will the production run rates be known?
- Who will be responsible for triggering contingency plans to the what-if analyses?

Master Data Management

This is, unfortunately, the less sexy areas of product portfolio management, but accurate and timely master data are crucial in product development—no data, no product. Figure 3.7 shows the primary data masters that are needed for the system to effectively plan and schedule a product in a manufacturing and distribution business.

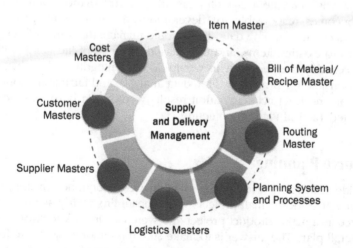

FIGURE 3.7 Master Data Requirements for Launch

Source: Oliver Wight. Copyright Oliver Wight International, Inc. Used with permission.

The primary data masters include the *item/material master, bill of material*, work-center profile, and routings, but there are other areas that might come into play depending on the nature of the supply chain, such as capacities, distribution, customer segmentation, and supplier data master. Data need a formal and rigorous management process to ensure timely and accurate planning parameters in the system. Some of these issues could be minor or easy-to-do projects, but experience has shown that there still needs to be a level of formality to them, and an assessment of the resource is needed to complete them on time.

For example, there is a rule of thumb that the product portfolio team creates the item or product originally, so it naturally follows they need to manage the changes from there on. This thinking, however, could cause a few problems. In one pharmaceutical company, there were enough of what they called "black label changes" to be a nuisance. Black label changes are minor changes to a label, such as an address or telephone number. With the way pharmaceutical companies were merging, acquiring each other, and changing their names at that time, there were hundreds of changes occurring at the same time, but they were seen as minor and originally excluded from the product portfolio remit. However, after an investigation of the root causes of why the total product plan was notorious for running late and causing increasing costs of material write-offs, as well as materials running out before the new labels arrived, it was found the minor changes were consuming so much resource that there was little time for anything else.

A more appropriate way to manage data for new and existing products and items is to create a cross-functional data governance team. This team then becomes responsible for developing and maintaining processes to ensure accurate planning data. They would manage the listing of new items, changes to existing items, and the phaseout of end-of-life items. Although not necessarily the people who would do data-integrity audits, they would be responsible for process design, data analysis, and facilitating continuous improvement. Data accuracy audit results would then be published in the Integrated Tactical Planning meeting.

Resource Planning

The hidden problem with all the small changes mentioned in the previous section is that those small projects were consuming nearly as much people resource as a major product project and were causing a knock-on effect on the overall plan. The answer is to make sure the minor projects are formally included in the pot of product projects and assessed for consumption of resource along with all the other projects and then formally included in the Integrated Tactical Planning process for monitoring of execution to plan.

Figure 3.8 shows a time-phased plan that assesses resource load by project category, matched against demonstrated capability. Resource planning starts at an aggregate monthly plan level, reviewed in the Integrated Business Planning process, and then gets broken down into weekly buckets for the Integrated Tactical Planning process to view and manage. It is recommended that a project management tool be used to guide each project. There are many benefits to using a project management tool, but one of them is that because they are date-driven, the resource can be viewed at a monthly, weekly, or daily level to check on load.

The behavioral response needs to be "silence is approval" in that it is assumed that the projects are being managed within the allocated resources and are on track, unless notified otherwise. If there is an issue, it will be raised through the central project forum or weekly meeting. Issues can arise from anywhere, such as from customer-driven specification changes, the project team capability, the manufacturing capability, or supplier ability to supply. Prioritization rules agreed through the Integrated Business Planning process should be passed through to the execution teams and used to guide decision-making.

If the execution teams can manage with the resource plan agreed at a monthly level, then use this plan. If certain bottleneck resources need more detailed planning, then translate the monthly resource plans into weeks and even days inside the planning time fence.

This will be particularly important for seasonal businesses and might require these factors:

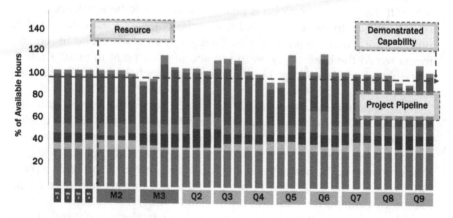

FIGURE 3.8 Resource Planning

Source: Oliver Wight. Copyright Oliver Wight International, Inc. Used with permission.

- A detail plan (even to a daily level) during the high season, then weekly inside the planning time fence.
- Extending the planning time fence for part of the year; for example, a client who manufactures ice cream extends their normal planning time fence from 12 to 18 weeks as summer approaches to cover the preseason build and to monitor postseason inventory draw off.
- If there is spare time, then considering whether there is an opportunity to pull forward production; for example, the production of Easter eggs can be done most of the year round and still stay within shelf life.
- Alternating supply sourcing between local and the other hemisphere.

The key point is that no plan should be approved if it is more than 100% loaded. Indeed, even a 100% loaded plan is dangerous in that there is no room for anything to go wrong. Based on history, it is always prudent to plan for less than 100% so that unforeseen changes can be accommodated. Consumption of that capacity should then be prioritized through the Integrated Tactical Planning process.

Another issue is working with the demand plan and time frames of visibility. In one food company that had many customer-driven new products the final demand plan was not shared with the supply side of the business until virtually it was on the production line being made. When challenged as to why they didn't provide a time-phased demand plan before the planning time fence, their response was that the customer hadn't given it to them . . . and there were no rules agreed with the customer about when a firm forecast should be shared with the team.

This gives rise to a brief diversion about what is communicated and when. If the product portfolio is healthy, there should be a balanced number of projects in each stage, and hence the emergency launches of new products should be minimized. That then goes to ask what kind of requirements would the business need to see and at what point in time? There is probably other terminology, but the terms that may help frame the thinking are *open, fuzzy,* and *firm.*

The *open* forecast is just that. It is usually before the funnel, or in the first stage, and probably in annual volume buckets. It will not be driving anything in a planning sense, and among other uses, it would be there to assess the health of the funnel. During the second stage, plans might be time phased over the next 3 years, but still not be driving anything in a planning sense. At the third gate, however, and hence moving into third stage, the forecast should be loaded in the system as *fuzzy,* using ghost SKUs (or a similar technique). It would still not be driving anything, but it is there for visibility and to run scenarios and capability tests, such as rough-cut capacity planning for critical resources and assessment of sales and distribution capability.

At the fourth gate, the plans become *firm* and the organization starts working with it as being real. It will be included in the demand planning system. The planning data is confirmed, it is being used for financial roll ups, and it is formally being driven by the master supply planning process— for all intents and purposes, it's happening. Also included in the demand plan should be trials, pipeline inventory builds, and any forecast cannibalization of existing products.

The fifth gate, should then be no less than the planning time fence used for Integrated Tactical Planning. In other words, once approval to produce and launch is given, the time frame for launch *should not be less than the planning time fence*. Some have argued that we don't understand the nature of business and that imposing a time fence on an approved new product launch is an opportunity cost to the business. I agree it is, but what is the cost of rushing the process and taking shortcuts? We have seen huge air-freight costs of key materials, lost inventory, specification mistakes, wrong pricing, and dissatisfied customers. The other risk often ignored is putting the priority on the potentially unknown new-product production at the expense of the known in-market products.

This is not to dismiss that the launch process should not be a focus for *velocity* improvements. It should, but velocity improvements come from a deliberate *Lean* deployment program, which is quite different to just saying "Go faster."

What is also useful to do is to map what is required by and for whom at each stage in the funnel. We have discussed fuzzy and firm demand plans, but there are also the other needs right through the gating process that require plans and information to be shared. For example, in the fourth stage, the supply team will need to have a forecast of requirements for running a trial. Similarly, the demand team will want to understand throughput or potential run rates to understand overhead allocation and the implication on margin. At the fourth gate, it is highly recommended that a must-meet criterion should be to run simulations of various scenarios, supported by contingency plans, to prepare for uncertainty. In this context how are they going to be generated, by whom, and who needs to know?

Once this is mapped out, it can be folded into the gate criteria and stage templates to ensure the knowledge is captured in process.

Project Management

As part of a robust product portfolio management process, project management is a critical element. It is expected that all product projects are formally and adequately resourced and there's a governance structure in place. This should be a must-meet criterion at the first gate.

As shown in Figure 3.9, the product master plan outlines the overall plan, but each project will need a project plan itself in sufficient detail to cover requirements for the Integrated Tactical Planning process.

Companies sometimes appoint a project management office (PMO) to manage everything project in the business, which in our experience has not been overly successful. The reason is that it becomes all too easy to abrogate responsibilities to the PMO and, if we were being cynical, assign blame to the PMO when things go wrong. However, to help make the PMO work for the business, leadership is needed in driving processes integrity, optimizing the use of the tool sets, and capturing and sharing the knowledge of best approaches.

There was a study published about the ability for projects to hit their milestone and due dates, which compared experienced project managers with inexperienced managers. Interestingly, the inexperienced managers had a much better track record of delivering projects on time than the more experienced managers. The reason postulated was that the experienced project manager had less expectations of delivering on time due to their years of missing deadlines, where their less experienced colleagues didn't know that most projects run late. The challenge, however, is to instill a sense of discipline and expectation into the project planning that milestones will be delivered on time at least 95% of the time.

People in organizations tend to get used to setting up a project that looks good on paper but find within a few periods from kickoff that it starts to lag. All looks well at the beginning, but as the launch or due dates get closer, a syndrome develops called *milestone creep,* which eventually becomes *milestone crunch,* and it's a sign of poor project management discipline. One global IT lead commented recently on a draft project plan, "Your plan looks pretty, but you're not going to hit even your most conservative launch date. Our company just doesn't value effective project management and turn a blind eye to not honoring the resources that are promised."

The following are some of the causes of this problem:

- Scope creep, which is when there are more things being added as the project goes on—sometimes because the team hadn't thought of it in the beginning and sometimes because senior management want the team to "do more with less"
- Poor resource planning—many companies don't plan resources at all and expect people to just juggle whatever comes at them
- Reinventing the wheel syndrome—every project starts as a blank slate and the learnings from previous projects are not considered when building the new project plan
- Poor cadence—the project team should be meeting weekly, but either the organization doesn't stipulate that this is the appropriate cadence, or for a multitude of reasons people don't turn up, meetings get postponed or cancelled, or the vicissitudes of the business cause ongoing distractions

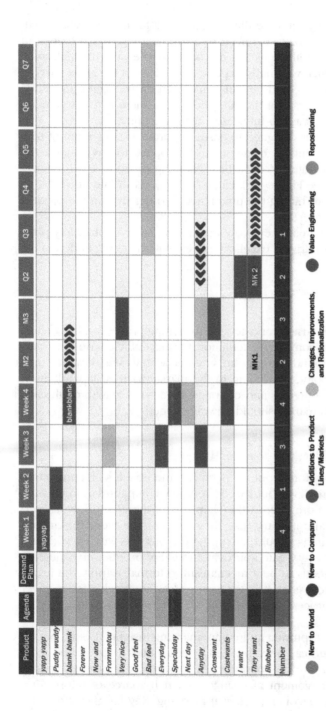

FIGURE 3.9 Master Product Plan

Source: Oliver Wight. Copyright Oliver Wight International, Inc. Used with permission.

The point is that by the time the project gets into the Integrated Tactical Planning process horizon, we need to avoid handing over a crunch of activities. There are several things that can be done to ensure that milestone crunch is avoided, which we briefly explore next. Many of the areas covered in the following sections could be considered part of the bigger Integrated Business Planning process, but like all other plans, there is that execution phase that is highly relevant to Integrated Tactical Planning.

The gating process is designed to ensure rigorous management of new product introductions, but the concept can be applied to any major activity or project. For the Integrated Tactical Planning process, it will engage in the second stage (see Figure 3.6), albeit the projects should be visible to the process well before hitting the time fence through sharing the product master plan (see Figure 3.9).

In addition to the areas previously mentioned, such as capability planning, the other keys to driving excellence in execution are expanded in the next sections.

Gate Criteria

Rigorously define the must-meet criteria in the gating process with objective criteria that meet the company's definition of success. Generic templates and criteria can be found through an internet search, but they are only useful as a starting point. If winning in the marketplace is dependent on a company's unique strategies and offerings, then what gets through each gate and ultimately to market should be well aligned.

Use Critique and Feedback

We hear a lot of discussion about the need for, and benefits of, conducting rigorous postlaunch reviews, but we see very few companies doing it well. We will discuss this more later in the chapter, but there is a downside to postlaunch reviews, and it is just that: they are post the event. To circumvent that delay, learnings should be captured along the way by adding a critique section after every gate approval and every product management review. There then needs to be a mechanism to formally apply the learning back into the process as it is captured. Also, feedback should cover more than just the process; it needs to cover people and behavior, process, and tools.

In a related area, capturing and communicating insights is often poorly done. The term *insights* can often be seen by companies as an ad hoc activity, or something that is done periodically. However, the product control process, and the management of change, is a rich source of information to integrate back into becoming better at planning. Key insights should be formally captured through the process each week and published monthly in the Integrated Business Planning process, via the product management review. Over time this will improve the quality and validity of the product portfolio plans.

For example, we have seen these insights lead to following:

- More precisely defining time to market and hence getting much better at hitting launch dates.
- Understanding and publishing more pertinent key metrics for the launch phase.
- Creating a more specific inventory policy and product-portfolio management process, including the D-for-delete process.
- More precisely and effectively managing write-off of finished goods and raw materials.
- Improving the forecast accuracy of new products and associated inventory availability.
- Customer delivery performance improvements for new products.
- Agreed decision rights on management of the whole portfolio.

Continually Developing the Tool Sets

We mentioned a few benefits of using proper project management software and here is another one. At the conclusion of each project, through the postlaunch review process, the latest, most successful project should be genericized and updated with the latest learnings. Key elements, such as refining definitions of roles and responsibilities, honing the time taken to complete each task, validating elapsed time between tasks, and tightening key decision points, can all be tightened each time a project is completed. It follows, therefore, that a must-meet criterion at gate one has to be, "Has the latest generic project plan been reviewed and applied to this project?"

One pharmaceutical company we worked with had a set of generic project plans to cover major projects, minor projects, and the three major channels they went to market through, which were pharmaceutical, over-the-counter, and supermarkets (see Figure 3.10 for a high-level example). All that was needed in preparation for the first gate must-meet criterion was to do the following:

- Put the start date in the project plan, which would then give a draft of dates for each activity and milestone thereafter.
- Change the names of roles and responsibilities and their percentage of time allocated to product management, which create the *resource profile* for the individual project and the rolled-up aggregate level.
- Add in and adjust for the nuances of this new project.

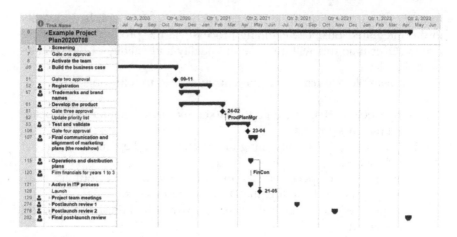

FIGURE 3.10 Example High-Level Project Plan

This not only saves project teams an enormous amount of time but also it creates a consistent platform and approach to managing the project, especially once the project hits the Integrated Tactical Planning process time fence.

Simulations at Gate Four

One of the must-meet criteria at the fourth gate we'd recommend is a set of simulations to model various possible scenarios leading up to and post the launch. This should be supported by preapproved contingency plans so that they can be efficiently executed if needed. These are usually part of the overall business plan, but they need to be interpreted and defined as trigger points to communicate when to enact. Examples of areas that some of our clients have used simulations for and hence driven the creation of a set contingency plans, are as follows:

- Distribution pipeline fill is more or less than the plan.
- Production run rates are more or less than the trials.
- Off-take is more or less than the plan.
- Price is more or less than the plan.
- Repeat purchase is more or less than the plan.
- Competitor retaliation is more or less than anticipated.

There is no doubt that there are many more examples, but as one senior manager was heard saying, "Most project managers hate modeling the possible alternatives, but we know that no project goes exactly to plan. However, once it has been done and the benefits of how swiftly we can respond and deploy the contingency plan are known, it is hard to go back to just putting up one plan and hoping everything goes to that plan."

Postlaunch Review and Gate Critique

For many of our clients, the postlaunch review is the final gate, which makes it just about impossible not to do. Depending on the type of organization, we would recommend conducting mini postlaunch reviews at approximately the first, second, and third quarters after launch, and then a final overall one at the 12-month mark, which is usually when the product classification is transferred from an N for new product to its BAU product classification such as A, B, or C.

Many companies who do postlaunch reviews confine it to comparing business plan results, for example, financials, volume, and sometimes market share. We recommend that it is more encompassing and includes these elements:

- **Project management,** including resource management, risk and opportunity planning, *change control*, budget control, quality management, systems and status reports, and technology support.
- **Process design and definitions,** including standard templates, generic project plans, rigor in gate criteria, decision-making, the data base, and communication.
- **Assumption performance,** including volume, market share, advertising reach, spend, PR effectiveness, price, and margin.
- **The plan at gate two** and comparison to actual results.

One client told us that the first time they did this they just used a simple quadrant consisting of feedback on these questions:

- What to start doing . . .?
- What to stop doing . . . ?
- What to do more of . . . ?
- What to do less of . . . ?

She said, "The 'aha' moment for me was when I reviewed the PLC (postlaunch review) document for a new project just 3 months later as specified in the first gate must-meet criteria, and I was shocked at how much I'd forgotten about that last project in such a short space of time. I'm a convert and have now developed a much more comprehensive set of PLR criteria."

Launch Preparedness

It seems that many projects are just left to be driven by one person at the later stages of development and launch approvals. Some of the issues we often see close to launch are as follows:

- New products being kept confidential until the last possible moment.
- Rushing to get to market as soon as possible and taking short cuts, skipping gate-approval criteria, and not doing the due diligence in scenario planning.
- Pet projects getting through to launch.
- Sales forecasts not being updated routinely enough to reflect the current reality leading up to launch, or launch volumes being artificially high to meet a hurdle rate in the approval process.
- Trials getting bumped for high-volume SKUs, usually driven by overhead recover and/or the bird-in-the-hand thinking.
- Late planning of pipeline build inventory.
- Lack of what-if analyses and agreement on the contingency plans to support the what-if analyses.
- Numerous postlaunch specifications changes.
- Unforeseen quality and technical issues.
- Losing interest postlaunch with no formal postlaunch reviews done and hence a loss of learning.

A lesson learned from neuroscience is that checklists do matter and do help with consistency in deployment. We don't have space here to go into the science of behavior modification but suffice it to say that standard gate templates and checklists will improve the deployment of project plans. They don't have to be overly complicated, as Figure 3.11 shows. It is a simple launch-readiness set of questions, which makes sure nothing is missed.

The only stipulation is that they must be used and must be formally checked off. If it is good enough for pilots and surgeons to use to keep us safe from mistakes, it is good enough to keep the lifeblood of the organization well managed.

The important point is that there needs to be a continuum of development and approvals, driven by rigorous adherence to the gate must-meet criteria, and a binary mindset of either approve to move on to the next stage or reject. Although it seems common sense to send a project back for rework, all it does is train the project lead to be sloppy in the preparation for gate approvals.

The Launch: Getting Ready

- Early production: how much, when?
- Full-scale production: where to make, how much, when?
- How to market the launch product?
- Deploying product early: when?
- Physical logistics: storage considerations.
- Brand marketing plans
- Effect on product category plans
- Customer plans
- Short-term targets, revenue, earnings, growth
- Pricing/service/invoicing
- Tracking customer acceptance and experiences
- Contingency plans: high/low sales, high/low production

FIGURE 3.11 Launch Checklist

Source: Oliver Wight. Copyright Oliver Wight International, Inc. Used with permission.

Summary and Key Change Requirements

In this section we have covered the key elements of product control and execution as it relates to the Integrated Tactical Planning process. The key definitions that need to be agreed on in advance are *product, new,* and *portfolio,* without which, the management of execution will be compromised.

A key player in the process, and member of the quorum of four, is the product project manager, who is responsible for representing the product plans in the process. The key elements of the product plan are managing the execution of the portfolio strategy, which includes new products, changes to existing products, and deletions. At the heart of the execution of a *new product introduction* is the stage-and-gate process. The process needs to be constructed using the company's definition of success, and the gate criteria need to be objective and have rigorous adherence.

It is vital that there is a capability planning process to understand the project load on the business and the doability of the product plan. It is also highly recommended that a project-planning tool be used to manage the product plan, including the resource plan.

Finally, more than any other part of the business, there's a balance between process rigor and discipline and being flexible. Capturing and applying the learning is fundamental for creating replicable processes but needs to be supported by simulation modeling to be ready for the inevitable uncertainty.

If we bring this all together through the Integrated Tactical Planning process, we find this excellence in execution means we win in the marketplace.

PEOPLE AND BEHAVIOR CHANGES

- A product project manager is needed to manage the execution of the product plans.
- Adherence to the gate criteria is critical.
- Understand that not all projects are equal with regard to resources load, management, and reward.
- Manage the not-launch-before time fence rigorously.

PROCESS CHANGES

- Definitions of gate criteria need to be objective and aligned with the company's view of success.
- The product plan is more than new products—it includes portfolio analysis, product life cycle management, and management of the deletion of SKUs and associated materials.
- The stage-and-gate process is a funnel, designed to brutally eliminate projects that don't meet the criteria.
- Resource planning based on demonstrated capability is essential.

TECHNOLOGY CHANGES

- The ability to set up and manage ghost SKUs.
- Assessment of the product portfolio profitability.
- Project management software.
- Resource planning capability.
- Using the data in the planning modules in the system, not spreadsheets.
- Using simulation for modeling and assessing multiple futures.

CHAPTER 4

Optimizing the Go-to-Market Approach
Executing the Demand Plan

In this chapter, we will provide an overview of elements required to successfully execute the demand plan within an Integrated Tactical Planning process. We will share an overview of activities involving the commercial organization (sales, product, and marketing functions, for example). We begin by focusing on those activities that stimulate demand and reference the term *demand management* to delineate among those activities that are more strategic in nature, versus the tactics required to ensure that plans are in place to address changing demand patterns in the near term.

We will cover the following key concepts in this chapter:

- Demand creation
- Definition of demand management
- Role of demand execution manager
- Linking demand planning to demand execution
- Forecast consumption
- Demand segmentation
- Abnormal demand
- Demand monitoring
- Order promising
- Benefits of demand execution

A fully integrated demand management process provides organizations visibility into customer and market opportunities for enhanced revenue and profitability. The resulting demand plan requires a coordinated sales, marketing, and product management effort in communicating changes stemming from customer plans, including ensuring the documentation of assumptions as well as recognizing inherent risks and opportunities that might affect the most likely outcomes. Consensus-driven demand output includes updated volumes to drive supply chain activities, as well as value in the form of gross revenue and gross margin, for example, to help deliver business commitments. A hallmark of the process is alignment on priorities and required investments, revisited at a minimum monthly, over an entire 24-month-minimum planning horizon. As a result, companies can use demand management principles to successfully achieve strategic and business objectives, such as sustained growth, improved profitability, and customer satisfaction.

Demand Creation

Specific activities that fall to the sales and marketing group include planning demand, communicating demand, influencing demand, and managing/prioritizing demand. Planning demand includes those activities that involve more than simply producing a forecast—the organization may find value in using historical observations to understand the past but should always challenge what might be different going forward. It may be helpful to consider your own businesses, particularly in light of recent global events, when you are to ask yourself how often the past is likely to repeat itself. The composition and timing of demand going forward may be significantly different than last month, last quarter, and last year. Communicating demand refers to sharing and collaboration among internal and external stakeholders involved in the demand planning process, including production, internal, and external supply partners. This also involves members of the financial organization who can use the plans generated to help appraise financially for any impact on business gross revenue, margin, contribution margin, and earnings before interest, taxes, depreciation, and amortization (EBITDA), for example. Influencing demand involves the Five Ps (product, placement, pricing, promotion, people) in line with ongoing marketing activities, as well as concentrated sales efforts such as executing ongoing sales territory plans. In essence, demand management is a big job and requires a concerted effort between both a sales and marketing group, as well as a demand planning and/or demand manager to coordinate quantitative and qualitative data. These efforts are exemplified in Figure 4.1, underscoring that demand for products and services involves a series of coordinated, ongoing efforts.

Although considerable time, energy, and resources underpin demand plans, even the most rigorous and thorough plans are by nature imperfect. A less technical term applies as one deals with the here and now: reality! Consequently, changes in plans and their impact become even more acute

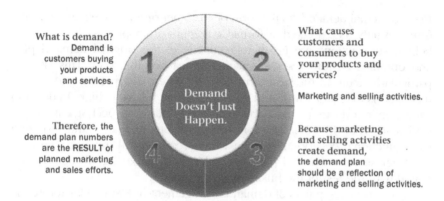

What is demand?
Demand is
customers buying
your products
and services.

What causes
customers and
consumers to buy
your products and
services?

Marketing and selling activities.

Therefore, the
demand plan numbers
are the RESULT of
planned marketing
and sales efforts.

Demand
Doesn't Just
Happen.

Because marketing
and selling activities
create demand,
the demand plan
should be a reflection of
marketing and selling activities.

Marketing and selling activities drive the forecast
or demand plan numbers, not the other way around.

FIGURE 4.1 Demand Doesn't Just Happen

Source: Oliver Wight. Copyright Oliver Wight International, Inc. Used with permission.

when there is less time available to formulate adequate responses including tactics needed to achieve the revenue assumed as part of the Integrated Business Planning process and maintain customer satisfaction. Consider the global pandemic of 2020 and the almost instantaneous changes in demand that affected a multitude of industries. No one could have imagined the impact these events would have across the globe. Although such a catastrophe may be considered to be highly infrequent and not likely to occur more than once in a lifetime, there are other real risks in domestic and global business dynamics that will continue to manifest themselves, reminding us that the only constant is change itself. The tactics to deal with this uncertainty and its impact on previously authorized demand plans will be front and center in this chapter. The process of demand management, when employed consistently, can help highlight changes to plans and bring nimble responses for action, escalation, and decisions as part of a formal Integrated Tactical Planning process.

Definition of Demand Management

The process of demand management can be viewed through the lens of both *demand planning* and *demand execution* processes, the latter being a response to help business answer the question, "How should and can we respond when demand materializes differently to what was planned?"

Because actual demand (in the form of customer orders, for example) rarely forms exactly as expected, a formal communication process is needed to help ensure actions are taken to reconcile to the original demand plan and optimize customer service at the lowest possible cost. This issue is particularly acute in the near-term horizon, where alternatives and recommendations may feel scarce and costs for change relatively high. In demand execution, efforts are focused on the tactical window, respecting cumulative lead times (our 13-week example from previous chapters) and requiring cross-functional collaboration from various commercial functions, such as customer service, demand planning, sales, and marketing, all tightly integrated with the rest of the business.

These two key pillars of demand management in Figure 4.2 capture the importance of demand planning efforts, which are required to stimulate the timing and level of products and services consumed in the marketplace, as well as demand execution activities, which are focused on ensuring plans and resources are aligned as the time frame shifts from future months to the here and now.

The demand planning horizon is focused on the medium- to long-term horizon as part of the Integrated Business Planning process, a horizon of no less than 24 months with a rolling horizon. Strategic decisions including understanding and employing tactics to drive demand typically dominate discussions in this time frame, drawing from multiple inputs of information that include statistical analysis, marketing intelligence, and product life cycle changes. Sales input, customer collaboration, as well as *strategic initiatives* are also considered and integrated. As mentioned

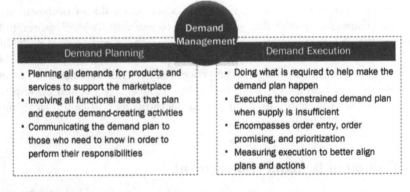

FIGURE 4.2 Definition of Demand Management: Demand Planning Versus Demand Execution

Source: Oliver Wight. Copyright Oliver Wight International, Inc. Used with permission.

previously in Chapter 3, in the near-term Integrated Tactical Planning horizon the type of information that is reviewed is more granular and revisited more frequently, usually in weeks instead of months. Changes are expected to occur and require immediate responses, albeit daily and weekly detailed must still be connected to the monthly activities of Integrated Business Planning. To reinforce this point, the use of the Integrated Planning model as depicted previously (Figure 2.1) is once again a helpful guide to illustrate the types of activities that dominate discussion in the execution layer. In Figure 4.3, the pertinent focus of demand execution activities are highlighted in green highlighting conversations and activities that dominate the below-the-line detailed area, all the while integrated with product and supply execution disciplines to ensure Integrated Tactical Planning is fully cross-functional, collaborative, and functioning to deliver a unified business response.

Activities highlighted under the demand review graph box in the center of this graphic represent the ongoing activities connected to aggregate demand planning, and they are visible as part of the Integrated Business

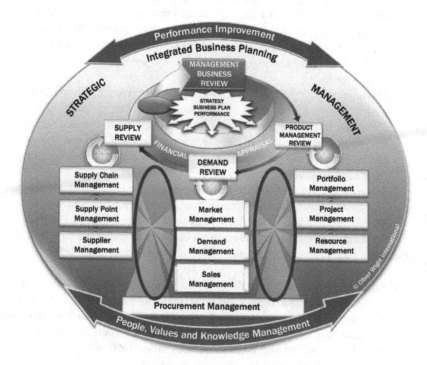

FIGURE 4.3 Below-the-Line Demand Execution Activities

Source: Oliver Wight. Copyright Oliver Wight International, Inc. Used with permission.

Planning process. They also cover detailed activities that are present in a demand execution process. One example of such activity would be a review of regular sales pipeline activity, the output of which feeds a monthly aggregate demand review but also is integrated into demand execution. Note also that similar to product execution, successful deployment involves integration across both product and supply as denoted by the circles indicating the links to product and supply activities.

There are specific areas to emphasize and provide additional detail to help define the scope of what needs to be considered in demand execution:

- Market management—promotional planning, competitive impacts, and monitoring of external factors that might affect execution:
  - Promotional planning—for those applicable industries in which planogram activities and promotional calendar assumptions over the next 6 to12 months are much different from the actual programs that are activated and executed.
  - Competitive impacts—understanding what competitors are doing in the marketplace either as a result of conscious efforts (taking share through recently launched new unique offerings) or what the marketplace is doing to them as a result of unplanned activities (for example, a rival plant failure), which can yield unexpected opportunities and/or risks.
  - Monitoring of external factors—global pandemics and hurricanes are nearly impossible to forecast precisely; however, employing scenarios derived from new information (assumptions) in the near term can be integrated into longer-term demand planning and the Integrated Business Planning process—extremely meaningful for business planning and replanning purposes.
- Demand management—demand planning involving statistical forecasting, analytics, artificial intelligence and related insights:
  - Statistical analysis—leveraging historical demand using algorithms in combination with segmentation techniques to integrate data and create a baseline view that may yield new information in the near term and long term.
  - Analytics—causal factors that can be leveraged (for example, impact of weather and pricing actions) that serve as a complement to strictly time series data in advanced models. In addition, many companies are also employing demand-sensing tools as a method to help capture the impact of significant changes aided through the availability of more powerful and inexpensive software.
  - Insights—demand managers/analysts are constantly asking what additional insights that can be gleaned from both qualitative and quantitative data.

- Sales management—pipelines, customers, and opportunities, for example, such as a customer using Integrated Tactical Planning to address opportunistic demand:
  - Pipelines—a professional sales and marketing organization typically employing an opportunity pipeline process, aided by customer relationship software in many instances (for example, Salesforce) to assess the relative size of funnel and actions to execute.
  - Opportunities as well as risks that tie directly into execution activities—having a client of the Integrated Tactical Planning process extremely focused on understanding not just which opportunities, for example, can be converted in the near term as they arise but also that these decisions are fully vetted and appraised financially with clear costs, visible trade-offs, and agreed to and aligned with supply chain for effective execution.
  - Demand execution and the Integrated Tactical Planning process helping to drive a forum for monitoring the pipeline, but also bringing clarity as to the decisions needed not just over the entire planning horizon but also to help address potential gaps to the committed Integrated Business Planning process plan wherever possible.

Following are some of the sales and marketing issues we often see that could affect an organization's ability to successfully execute:

- Customer ordering swings violently different than what was planned.
- The loss of a customer, the gain of a customer.
- Competitive threats that might lead to a sudden reduction in demand for another company's offerings.
- Competitive opportunities that may yield a sudden boom in demand for the same company.

Role of Demand Execution Manager

The demand execution manager is an important part of the quorum of roles described in Chapter 2. In some organizations, this role is part of the demand manager function, with a manager who has the bandwidth to oversee both product lines or categories, for example, as well as who can participate in weekly tactical meetings. In larger companies, the demand execution manager may fall to specific demand planners/analysts, who each serve specific product lines and categories and may also have regional responsibilities. This role is typically new when companies initially implement a demand execution process but is quickly seen as invaluable. Some specific activities performed by the demand execution manager are included in Figure 4.4.

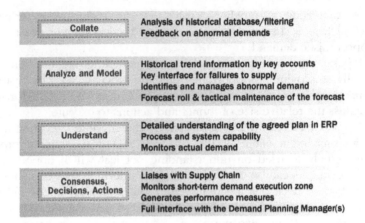

FIGURE 4.4 Demand Execution Manager Role

Source: Oliver Wight. Copyright Oliver Wight International, Inc. Used with permission.

The demand execution manager role consists of five primary elements:

- Liaising with order management regarding *order promising* and availability.
- Understanding how orders are being managed when demand exceeds available supply.
- Reporting and facilitating for when demand is materializing to be less than planned.
- Making decisions related to *forecast consumption*.
- Facilitating decision-making when demand materializes differently than planned.

As you can imagine, this role requires a person who communicates well cross-functionally with product managers, customer service, sales, marketing, demand planning, and supply planning. The person must also manage well up and down the organization and must be trusted by the commercial functional area leader. The person must also be comfortable working in the detail while also keeping the customer perspective and the company's well-being in mind.

Cross-functional collaboration on the part of sales is also needed to share relevant insights and knowledge with the demand execution manager. A sales organization should be embedded with its customers' wants and needs. Therefore, the sales group is also a reliable source of information about future customer requirements or any updates to the latest input required for the Integrated Business Planning process. Although some organizations feel beholden to customers and their apparent inability to forecast future demand requirements, a tightly orchestrated sales organization with support of a full-time demand execution manager helps identify changes in customer demand patterns, armed with the curiosity to constantly challenge customer assumptions, which must be documented and communicated when changes become significant for maximum business visibility.

One client's definition of responsibilities for sales are outlined here:

- Responding to demand execution manager's requests in a timely manner.
- Prioritizing decisions that are required among customers, brands, and channels.
- Understanding demand drivers for the abnormal demand events and feedback into the demand planning assumptions.

In summary, the demand execution manager is responsible for ensuring the demand plan is on track to meet the first 3 months (sample time frame inside the planning time fence) of the demand plan as agreed during the previous Integrated Business Planning cycle. In addition, as part of the quorum of key players in the broader Integrated Tactical Planning process, this role also helps to ensure that critical decisions and potential escalations are being appropriately documented and raised.

Linking Demand Planning to Demand Execution

To link demand planning to demand execution, the aggregate demand plan must be disaggregated to the execution level to enable supply planning to be effective and to allow for monitoring the execution of the demand plan during the month. In the previous section, we described the important role of the demand execution manager, who helps ensure the agreed plan as authorized through the IBP process is correctly reflected in the ERP system of record, for example. One concern is that if it is left at the aggregate level and in monthly buckets, this monthly aggregate demand doesn't facilitate effective execution, and all kinds of decisions needed to do so could be at risk. At the heart of an effective demand execution and ITP process is ensuring the appropriate level of detail exists; therefore, best practice demand management assumes that the timing, level, and composition of demand is an ongoing activity guided by time horizons.

The activity of disaggregating a monthly Integrated Business Planning demand plan into weekly buckets is depicted in Figure 4.5.

Without the use of advanced planning tools and/or other types of software, this endeavor can be quite challenging. Specifically, ERP software that provides the ability to view demand in weekly slices or buckets is

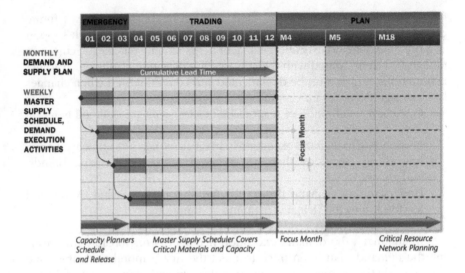

FIGURE 4.5 Aggregate Versus Detailed Demand Execution Activities—The Focus Period Ensuring Smooth Transition

Source: Oliver Wight. Copyright Oliver Wight International, Inc. Used with permission.

imperative, because giving visibility to weekly and sometimes even daily demand pacing is important in the tactical zone, compared to monthly views, of demand in the mid- to long-term Integrated Business Planning horizon. Many clients default to a simple approach where the monthly number is divided by the number of weeks for that month. This method is relatively simple and straightforward; the only watchout is that there might also be specific weeks (last week of the month) where orders are consistently more than other weeks so if true this assumption should be reflected and can be an exception to the previously noted 'straightline' approach.

Forecast Consumption

Once the demand plan is disaggregated at a weekly level, thought needs to be given into how incoming orders are netted off against this to give a view of the latest demand picture in the Integrated Tactical Planning horizon. The process by which a forecast (planned demand) is replaced by a customer order (actual demand) is referred to as forecast consumption. Orders are unlikely to be identical to the forecast, especially if disaggregation has been done using the generic logic described previously, and when this is the case, typically the ERP system is set to consume backwards and forwards against set criteria to net the order off against the forecast of a number of consecutive weeks. This avoids inflating or deflating the short-term demand and provides stability in the signals that this demand sends to the rest of the organization. However, it needs monitoring because it is too easy to leave a trail of unconsumed demand without understanding why or to forward consume too far into the future and fail to spot a problem looming on the horizon. We shall consider this in the *demand monitoring* section following. This is why you need a gating process at regular intervals to decide whether to reset the forecast consumption position. Visuals are a helpful guide here, and the example shown in Figure 4.6 highlights a weekly pacing report in which planned demand and actual demand are tracked. You will note that both the planned and actual quantities are in synch until week 4, when a decision needs to be made as to whether to consume the remaining forecast of 100 units or roll over this quantity to a future period to ensure sufficient product is available to meet requested demand. Most software systems have logic that can be programmed to account for how forecast is consumed and rolled—nothing, however, replaces human acumen and experience.

Regardless of the system used to view and compare data, we cannot lose sight of the value of documented assumptions. Integrated Tactical Planning can help drive decisions and actions by comparing what has changed from the time between the sign-off of the Integrated Business

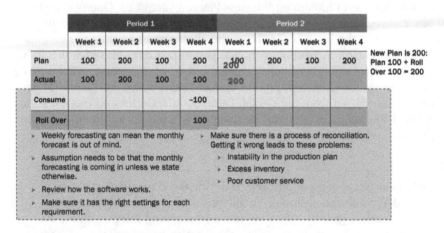

FIGURE 4.6 Forecast Consumption and Roll Logic—Ignoring It Can Trip You Up!

Source: Oliver Wight. Copyright Oliver Wight International, Inc. Used with permission.

Planning process plan and the subsequent reality materializing in the near term. Therefore, having a line of sight into what the original thinking was in the plan and being able to monitor these as documented assumptions in execution is important yet at the same time also often difficult. Most of the time we see the capturing of the changes in assumptions being done offline versus integrated into software; a significant opportunity exists from the author's perspective on integrated assumption management within most software systems to aid with documentation and facilitate improved ease of filtering on which assumptions have changed from prior period.

Human intervention and collaboration is, of course, fluid and crosses multiple time frames. Within this linking process in the tactical window, cross-functional collaboration including sales, demand planning, customer service, and supply functions work together to ensure the disaggregation from a customer grouping or family level to when the ship point/destination and product details are in place. This link ensures that the appropriate timing, level, and composition of demand is visible in order to be satisfied by the supply organization and that a feedback loop exists up to the demand execution manager on any changes in the breakdown of the aggregate plan as month 4 moves into month 3 in our planning horizon—the previously noted focus month.

Effectively linking demand-planning activities to execution decisions are part of the oversight of the demand manager. Similarly, ensuring new information in the form of assumptions, risks, and opportunities that can be brought forward as part of ongoing demand planning activities that feed the mid- to long-term Integrated Business Planning activities. One of our clients has a stated goal of using the output of the weekly execution meetings to better inform the business both for the short term and over the extended planning horizon. A benefit of the integrated processes includes the ability to have line of sight to what has changed, over what horizon, and knowing that changes are expected. From a demand perspective, at the end of each month, the output from the demand execution activities and the Integrated Tactical Planning process can be effectively used to inform the demand planning process.

"Demand execution introduced a formalized mechanism to effectively manage customer escalations and improve the long-term demand plan by capturing demand planning insights. Results included an improvement in demand plan accuracy by over 20% and an increase in customer satisfaction by nearly 40%."

Client Testimonial

Demand Segmentation

Throughout our description of the Integrated Tactical Planning process, we have attempted to reinforce the necessity to be able to extract meaningful detail to efficiently and confidently execute previously agreed Integrated Business Planning plans. The ability to do so requires adequate software, as well as trained professionals, who can cut through what may appear to be voluminous amounts of data and focus on exceptions that truly matter. Combine these factors with the author's experience that few organizations have unlimited resources, the task of assembling relevant data to focus on the critical few can be challenging, and knowing where to begin can be daunting—implementing it for all products/categories/items can at times feel overwhelming and burdensome. The early chapters of this book highlighted the use of Pareto analysis, which is well recognized and accepted as an effective model to help highlight the critical few factors that can be helpful in explaining the outcome of many. In this section we introduce the concept of demand segmentation and offer real client examples of the application of its techniques.

Demand segmentation or stratification is an effective and efficient method to highlight the critical few customers/categories/items, particularly when faced with a significant number of SKUs and trying to determine which of these need attention. This methodology also affords more opportunity to focus on those SKUs, such as new products, which may require more effort and deserve more time. Segmenting demand according to volume and variability can often prove invaluable. A well-known technique is the use of the A, B, C methodology that was described in Chapter 2. Demand segmentation affords the demand team the opportunity to focus on the critical few items driven by business criticality. It also allows for effective use of resources, given that some organizations may not only have hundreds of items but several or tens of thousands.

We should reinforce that some clients have a well-defined customer service policy, with strategic customers identified and segmentation of these customers and key products and offerings identified relative to overall revenue and/or margin contribution. Service failures impacting customers will be acutely felt so in addition to incorporating service as a potential Key Performance Indicator, using a Customer Service Policy to help guide potential customer prioritizations (service targets and even potetntial allocations for example) can be illustrative. An example of segmentation is visible in Figure 4.7. This example highlights an approach that can be both effective and scalable as you pilot and eventually implement Integrated Tactical Planning across multiple segments or locations. Examples include specific items (A items, for example) versus wholesale business segment demand plans, which are important to monitor but more relevant to outside of the Integrated Tactical Planning horizon. One client has effectively used this

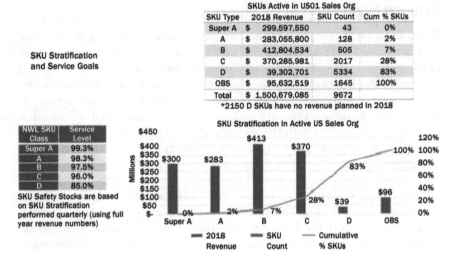

FIGURE 4.7 Example of Demand Segmentation Techniques

Source: Oliver Wight. Copyright Oliver Wight International, Inc. Used with permission.

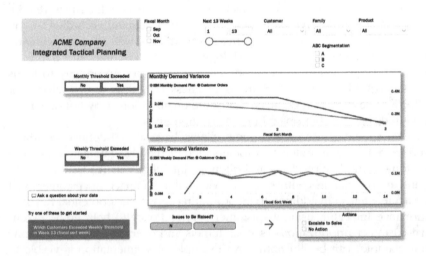

FIGURE 4.8 Use of Data Visualization Techniques in Demand Execution

Source: Oliver Wight. Copyright Oliver Wight International, Inc. Used with permission.

approach by combining both a product hierarchy lens (A, B, C items) as well as customers (A, B, C) to help size the problem and resulting conversation as part of their demand execution activities. This highlights an example of how another client drove what was truly meaningful as the client focused on key items with impact tied to service objectives. Figure 4.7 is an example of segmenting SKUs into ABCD groupings and the expected behaviors, such as keeping A SKUs service levels at 99+% but not being too concerned with D SKUs at 85%.

Abnormal Demand

Integrated Tactical Planning is focused on highlighting exceptions and the significant impact these deviations may have from what was agreed to as part of the Integrated Business Planning process. A key trigger for initiating demand exceptions as part of the demand execution activities is the deviation of actual demand (requested product or actual customer orders) compared to planned demand (volumes, revenue that were accounted for in the demand plan) and making an informed, best-for-business decision about how to proceed.

Variances in demand should be expected and actions routinely taken to understand the root causes and assumptions behind demand that failed to materialize as planned. However, some variances between planned demand and actual demand are so impactful to the business that they may be interpreted as abnormal and need special consideration and an immediate response. Examples of abnormal demand include a large customer order that was not anticipated and not in the demand plan, or it was anticipated in the demand plan but the actual demand that lands inside the planning time fence is significantly higher than originally planned as a result of a customer expanding operations or product lines. Each company will have its own definition based on the impact, disruption caused, and consequences, but the key element is the process of identifying and generating agreement, often in a relatively short period of time. Abnormal demand serves as a trigger for a potentially larger business issue and helps size the magnitude of potential issues for escalation and decisions (see Figure 4.9). Aligning and agreeing on the definition of demand enables the organization to be focused on what is truly critical versus the normal level of variation, because no forecast will ever be perfect. We have seen organizations invest significant resources in people and software to improve forecast accuracy, yet when confronted with the reality that some level of natural variation is expected, they often neglect the importance of agreeing on what level of variation really is unexpected, unaccounted for, and should be mitigated. Agreeing on a definition

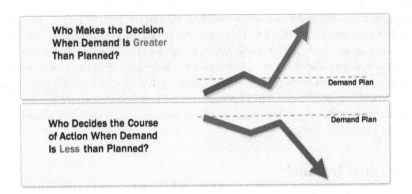

FIGURE 4.9 Abnormal Demand: Demand Execution Consists of a Decision-Making Process

Source: Oliver Wight. Copyright Oliver Wight International, Inc. Used with permission.

of abnormal demand avoids paralyzing the organization and wasting time on natural deviations in demand given that agreed tactics should also be in place, such as safety stock, to help address some variation and the ability of the organization to successfully respond.

Abnormal demand can have different tolerances depending on the level of detail involved (business segments, product lines, or individual SKUs). It should be noted as well that abnormal demand can occur equally in make-to-stock, make-to-order, assemble-to-order, and engineer-to-order environments. In one heavy project-based business we helped, the company employed demand execution techniques by establishing abnormal demand triggers related to quotes and tenders that could be several months into the future. This business was able to quickly identify significant changes in assumed demand and by highlighting those that were particularly large and not anticipated, rally the organization around the options to serve, even with relatively short lead times. Abnormal demand is dependent on your business definition of demand, and this can vary across entities. One client, as a starting point, put the company's best foot forward with a draft statement that simply read "Abnormal demand—customer orders that are outside of the normal range assumed in planning." Again, this needed to be refined but simply having some parameters to start with fostered a discussion regarding what "normal" means and, of course, how that might vary from one customer, product line, or SKU across their entire portfolio.

Regardless of business or industry, a simple definition of *abnormal demand* should include a reference that it is "a significant variance from the demand plan." This also infers that a company should have a procedure that states the process and mechanism for identifying abnormal demand at the point of order receipt and a policy for dealing with abnormal demands in providing service to customers.

Examples of abnormal demand include the following:

- New customer.
- New ship-to location.
- Significant quantity for that item.
- Significant quantity for that customer.

Note also that abnormal demand can occur as a single event or can be cumulative.

When done well, an effective execution process helps the organization manage imbalances between demand and supply by prioritizing demand to optimize customer service, profitability, and inventory investment when available supply of products and/or services cannot be synchronized with the volume, timing, and/or mix of demand agreed to as part of an Integrated Business Planning process.

When a demand execution process is not in place or decision-making boundaries are not well defined, the sales and marketing organizations do not have a chair at the table for aligning on needed decisions. There is also the tendency that needed escalations are surfaced to the most senior salesperson, which is not a best practice; rather approval guidelines should be clear and in line with responsibility and authority (sales manager, director, etc.). At the end of the day, the involvement of sales often results in a change of behavior by the supply chain planning organization, which may not be accustomed to allowing the sales leadership to determine which customers will receive product when demand is greater than supply.

Demand Monitoring

We have previously discussed how forecast consumption looks at the consumption of orders against the forecast and how abnormal demand identifies the spikes. The ability to monitor these and other variations in demand and highlight those that are true exceptions for potential review and escalation is central to a demand execution process. In Figure 4.10, a simple forecast denoted by 25 units per week is compared to a variance threshold with actions to support. The intention is to have tolerances for what is normal, and the intent is to react only when you breach the normal threshold. This ability to review such changes by week and identify which are a true variance may be supported by software systems and reporting. One client we worked with leverages system capability to flag variances by week,

	Period 1	Period 2	Period 3	Period 4
Action	Mark for attention.	Look to increase forecast.	Make sure you understand.	Make sure that the why is understood because it may affect the following weeks and months.
+	40	70	90	
Forecast	25	50	75	100
-	15	30	50	Roll or not? Make sure that the why is understood because it may affect the following weeks and months.
Action	Mark for attention.	Look to decrease forecast.	Make sure you understand.	

FIGURE 4.10 Monitoring Demand: Daily/Weekly Demand Variance Monitoring

Source: Oliver Wight. Copyright Oliver Wight International, Inc. Used with permission

enabling the demand execution manager, in collaboration with customer service, to monitor closely potential actions. Many clients still rely on an offline reporting system to download the monthly demand plan and separate into weekly buckets. Note that some may actually be forecasting in weekly buckets versus monthly; in this instance you are assuming there is intelligence and supporting assumptions to plan at this level, but you could simply use the actual forecast by week and compare it to the actual demand as it materializes. The beer industry does this down to a daily level, where it understands the normal flow of orders through a week and re-replenish bars driven by the spike in consumption over the weekend. Whatever your demand pattern is, the key is to know what is normal so that you can then identify when something deviates from this.

Whenever a variance does occur, it is important to understand the root causes. Tracking variances to plan becomes less about looking back and more about using a proactive approach to understand what it means for the future.

Order Promising

Another important activity that falls within the responsibility of the demand organization with a link to demand execution is that of order promising and flow. The demand monitoring process discussed previously looks to understand the rate and composition of actual demand in the form of customer orders in relation to the demand plan agreed in the latest Integrated Business Planning cycle. Where the demand was anticipated the expectation would be that you can satisfy that demand, but, unfortunately, we all know that this is not always the case. And so, each individual order line needs to be checked, either automatically or manually, against the latest supply position to ensure that a valid promise is given and maintained throughout the order life cycle. Various functions, such as customer service and supply, may be heavily engaged in the transactional details of order management, and the demand execution manager plays an important facilitation role working closely with all concerned to resolve issues and prioritize the orders and ensure good communication throughout. We noted the importance of assumptions in the realm of demand management: in the activity of order promising, understanding original assumptions and commitments and the ability to ensure customer satisfaction is critical. Again, there is functionality in most ERP systems to support this (available-to-promise, or ATP), but this is an area where clients often say that the functionality doesn't work so they haven't used it. The logic and math behind it is simple, but the underlying requirement on master data and data integrity is high so the problem often lies in the discipline and rigor of the processes rather than the often-blamed tool capability.

Benefits of Demand Execution

Outputs of the demand execution process include a summary of the changes and any commentary about concerns raised in meeting the plan. In Chapter 7 we discuss the meeting and review structure in more detail to understand how this information will paint the overall picture of the Integrated Tactical Planning weekly process. Issues that cannot be resolved by the team or that cannot wait for the next cycle will be escalated to appropriate leadership for decisions and support. For those organizations in which silos are not the norm and communication flows freely and frequently today, great; keep on doing it! For those that wish to embark on a demand execution journey or who perhaps engage in some of the activities but in a less formal or consistent manner across locations and/or business segments, what we have described for you will aid in evolving and improving the groundwork you have laid.

Benefits of a well-run demand execution process include improved customer service results, increased sales revenue, and being respected as a reliable supplier. Bottom-line benefits are also experienced by many of our clients. For example, our experiences show that inventory reductions of as much as 25% and customer service improvement of a point or two will be reflected in a growth in revenue, operational, and other related parameters. When companies implement a demand execution process to complement their existing Integrated Business Planning process, the realization of these benefits is accelerated. An additional benefit may be less obvious but nonetheless very impactful – helping transition the focus of executives beyond near-term issues. By having processes running smoothly and in control, executives are kept informed and not dragged into the weeds. The company's executive leaders can truly concentrate on the future—4 months and beyond—and help ensure that the company has the resources to fulfill demand and grow the business.

Summary and Key Change Requirements

In this chapter we have covered the key elements of demand execution as it relates to the Integrated Tactical Planning process including abnormal demand, demand monitoring, and forecast consumption. At the heart of demand execution and a key trigger for understanding the significance of deviations in actual demand is line of sight to abnormal demand events. Definition(s) of abnormal demand, as well as tolerances defining thresholds, need to be clear and should include the associated level of detail that reference business, segment, and item-level details including location details where applicable and relevant.

The ability to recognize deviations to plans emphasizes the need to ensure a well-designed demand monitoring process is in place. Prerequisites include the ability to disaggregate the monthly demand plan into weekly buckets, with simplified reporting in place to compare these against actual demand. At a minimum, reporting systems (integrated or offline software) must be able to provide visibility to the detailed plan sufficient for analysis and decision-making. We have seen significant evolution in the use of reporting tools, including the use of dashboards to convey key insights and afford the user the ability to drill into appropriate levels of detail—all fostering great discussion and framing potential decisions.

A key player in the process is the demand execution manager, who is responsible for representing the demand plan in the process. Important elements of the demand plan include managing the execution of the sales and marketing strategy, which includes leveraging statistical and analytical tools, as well as understanding the impact of changes tied to portfolio (additions, deletions), customer patterns, pricing, competition, and other external factors.

As noted in the product execution section, ensuring a manageable balance between the appropriate level of visible information for decision-making and not making the demand execution process more complicated than necessary is a primary goal. Sufficient learnings through piloting, which will be captured in upcoming chapters in this book, will assist with lessons learned and continuously evolving and improving the demand execution process.

If we bring this all together through the Integrated Tactical Planning process, this excellence in execution means we win in the marketplace.

PEOPLE AND BEHAVIOR CHANGES

- A demand execution manager role is needed to manage the execution of the demand plans.
- Recognition that deviations in actual customer demand versus planned demand are to be expected, and not all variances to plan need to be reviewed, discussed, or become potential candidates for escalations.
- Ability to focus on the vital few is aided by segmentation techniques.

PROCESS CHANGES

- An agreed definition (can vary by category, product line, item) of abnormal demand is critical.
- Changes to the agreed demand plan need to include an emphasis on what assumptions have changed, with supporting documentation and accountability as input into demand execution.
- A key deliverable of demand execution is confidence to meet intended demand plans, with underlying actions to support; it is not about reforecasting.

TECHNOLOGY CHANGES

- Enterprise software capability that supports disaggregating or decomposing a monthly demand plan into weekly views or buckets, from which actual demand (for example, orders and shipments) can be compared and viewed versus planned demand.
- Reporting capability that can include integrated software such as SAP, Oracle, and others as well as tools such as Microsoft Excel and Power BI that afford detailed analysis and data visualization view to illustrate segmented customers, products, items as well as KPIs.
- Software that supports a repository for documenting demand planning assumptions that is critical to understanding the difference between what was committed to in Integrated Business Planning process versus what is now visible in the demand execution process.

CHAPTER 5

Managing the Value
Supply Scheduling and Execution

As we move into the third of the three core plans, there is a distinct change in thinking. In the product area, the thinking is about effectively leveraging the opportunity to grow margin through future product portfolio plans. In the demand area, it is about optimizing the margin with existing products and customers. When we enter the realm of supply, it is about cost-effectively meeting those requirements in the business and also about ensuring alignment of the whole supply chain to drive competitive advantage. Typically, the Integrated Tactical Planning process will be at a supply point, or individual node of the supply chain, and will be at a deeper level of granularity than the Integrated Business Planning process; it could even be at a SKU or deeper subfamily level but still be governed by the overall supply chain strategy and plans coming out of the most recent Integrated Business Planning cycle.

The definition of *supply point* could be a *distribution center*, a manufacturing facility, a regional or global hub, or, for one of our clients, a product category level. In that category structure, it was convenient and coincidental that the manufacturing and distribution supply points were almost exactly aligned with the marketing categories, but, unfortunately, that is not such a common occurrence. We will share more on the potential matrix structures for consideration in the process design in Chapter 7.

We will cover the following key concepts in this chapter:

- Key aspects of supply execution.
- *Master supply planner/scheduler* as a pivotal role.
- Time fence management—the next level of detail.
- Stocking strategies.
- Decoupling demand and supply.

- Demonstrated capacity planning.
- Inventory management.
- Aligning the supply chain.

Key Aspects of Supply Execution

The overarching driver for supply planning and supply scheduling is the *master planning and scheduling* set of processes. This is covered in depth in the best book ever written on the subject, *Master Scheduling* (Proud, 2013), so we will not go into detail on that topic in this chapter, but we will explore the key elements as required for the Integrated Tactical Planning process. Suffice to say that the term *master* says it all—it is the master of all other supply plans and schedules.

Figure 5.1 is a preview of John Proud and Eric Deutsch's new book, *Master Planning and Scheduling,* which will be the fourth edition of the very successful *Master Scheduling* book. The interface among planning and execution processes and time periods will be topics of the rest of this chapter.

There are a number of fundamentals to understand first. Figure 5.2 expands on the key aspects of supply execution and, as can be seen, it is a broad set of activities. The overarching observations are that it is demand aligned, but not demand reactionary; it is cost-effective, but not overhead recovery driven; it is stability driven, but not rigidly fixed. It is, however, a

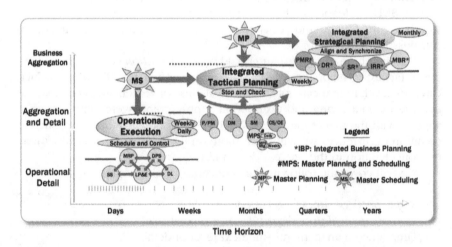

FIGURE 5.1 Integration of Master Planning and Scheduling with ITP and IBP

Source: Oliver Wight. Copyright Oliver Wight International, Inc. Used with permission.

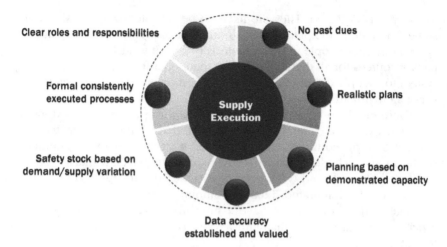

Clear roles and responsibilities

No past dues

Formal consistently executed processes

Supply Execution

Realistic plans

Safety stock based on demand/supply variation

Planning based on demonstrated capacity

Data accuracy established and valued

FIGURE 5.2 Key Aspects of Supply Execution

Source: Oliver Wight. Copyright Oliver Wight International, Inc. Used with permission.

set of principles that everyone in the business must sign up for—and not just supply chain and operations—and pave the way for open and honest communications and validity of planning, which can assist in driving increased competitive advantage.

Addressing **no past dues** might first appear to be a level of detail too deep to discuss in the executive's guide, but read on—it is more important than most people think. Read the heading as no *past-due orders*. A system order can be a sales order, a finished goods production order, a material order, a transfer order, or a purchase order. What it means is quite straightforward, and that is if we run a report on orders with a due date that is in the past, we should come up with nothing. Unfortunately, many companies don't have a formal past-due order maintenance process, and we have seen companies with orders (once the date filters are turned off) going back many months and sometimes years.

The problem is that a planning system cannot operate effectively with past-due orders. That is like arriving at the airport for a business trip, only to find out that you should have arrived at your destination yesterday—that is likely to cause a bit of panic and chaotic behavior trying to figure out what to do next!

You might be asking, how is it that companies can have data in the planning system that drives erroneous plans and still be using the planning system? The answer is simple: they aren't using the planning system for what it is designed. They are likely to be substituting spreadsheets for some, if not all, of the planning or ignoring the assistance that the planning system can offer people in doing their daily jobs. It is such a waste of company resources for all that money to be spent on a fit-for-purpose planning system for people to opt out and use spreadsheets, especially when the fix is not all that hard and just requires a little discipline.

There needs to be a past-due order clean-up process that is done at least weekly, and the simple solution is to redate all those orders to valid due dates or delete them. This aligns well with the weekly regeneration of the master schedule, which is the master supply plan that everyone needs to believe in and work to. It is also the critical supply set of plans that makes the Integrated Tactical Planning process work. The simple message is that you do not have a time machine and cannot perform a task in the past, so to maintain a valid plan, all dates have to be in the future.

Realistic plans and planning based on demonstrated capacity go hand in hand. The first is a mindset and the second is a process. Realistic plans mean just that—plans are achievable and reliable. In some companies there is a mindset that if you don't set stretch targets and goals, then people will not try hard enough. As discussed in Chapter 2, this is what is known as a logical fallacy, which sounds right and logical, but it could not be more wrong. Also, some companies set up targets and hope that they are achieved, but hope is not a strategy. Just because you would like to achieve something is not a reason to put it in the plan.

The way this is overcome is via a demonstrated capacity-planning process. We'll discuss this is more detail later, but in short, it means assessing what we have been able to demonstrate in the recent past and using that demonstrated performance as the foundation for the new plans, unless we know something different is going to happen, for example, putting on a new shift. In this case we would call it *planned demonstrated capacity*.

Following on from the past-due order discussion, the planning system will not work without accurate data. **Data accuracy must be valued** and processes put in place to ensure it is ongoing. There are two fundamental types of data and its associated accuracy:

- Static: this is data that doesn't change day to day, such as the ingredients in a food product, the steps that the manufacturing process goes through, or the types of products that a distribution center manages.
- Dynamic: as the names suggests, this refers to data that are changing all the time, such as the transactions capturing inventory movements or timeliness of transaction and order closures.

In a manufacturing environment, the key static master data are item (material) master, bills of material, routings, and *work center* files, and, in a distribution environment, the bills of distribution. In all physical goods environments, there will be *dynamic data* such as inventory record accuracy in which the transaction timeliness and accuracy is a critical factor; similarly in distribution environments, there are picking, packing, and shipping accuracy requirements. There are other files and data records in which data accuracy must similarly be established, such as supplier master data, customer master data, and price lists/product catalogs. The absence of accuracy for any one of these elements will reduce the effectiveness of the planning system. If all are missing, then quite frankly the system will be rendered useless and will not be trusted.

We are often asked about software and technology to make sure data remain accurate. There are many ways to error proof data entry in the software, such as running analysis routines on existing data and using bar scanners for the seamless recording of transactions. The issue is, however, that there must first be a mindset and set of processes that proactively scan master data files and fix errors before they affect the planning system. As a supply chain director said once, "I thought this was a crock of crap and there was nothing wrong with my people fixing errors when they found them, but when we—admittedly reluctantly—started proactively working through our master data, we uncovered errors that had been driving us crazy for years with aberrant plans, and this has ended up saving us not only a huge amount of chasing-up time, but has virtually eliminated reconciliation activity at budget time." Many business leaders are horrified when they discover the accuracy level, or rather inaccuracy, of their data. Even in highly regulated industries such as pharmaceutical companies, it is not unheard of to have a level of accuracy of less than 50% on something as critical as the bill of materials.

The key mindset changes to accomplish are listed here:

- Data management and accuracy needs to be proactive, not just a focus when there is a problem.
- Actively looking for errors is critical and needs to occur regularly.
- People need to be rewarded for accuracy.
- Errors are caused by poor processes and poor processes are caused by not understanding the value of the company's data—so the process needs to ensure that problems aren't just fixed, but that they uncover what caused them, and then design this out of your process.

On a broader issue, there is a lot of discussion about "big data," predictive modeling, machine learning, and AI, but if we can't get our fundamental planning data right to drive planning modules, how are we ever going to be able to trust futuristic algorithmically driven information?

Most supply chains have inherent uncertainty, and if you ask most supply chain and operations people, "Where does most of the 'noise' come from?" they are likely to say changes in demand plans and customer ordering patterns. The solution is usually to get the sales and marketing team to get better at forecasting, but that is only part of the answer. The full answer is to understand the errors in the forecast, and although we trust the sales and marketing team to be working on improving accuracy, we need the supply side of the business to be anticipating and planning for the variation.

One way to do this is via setting up **safety stock based on demand-supply variation**. We all know that inventory is there to protect us, but from what? Many companies adopt a one-size-fits-all approach to inventory based on the future coverage of the demand plan or a period of historical sales. This pot of inventory is then fair game to everyone to dip into for whatever issue or problem arises, whether that be unexpected orders, shortfall in production, or promotional opportunities. If there is no discipline, it causes frustration and conflict and often ends up with winners and losers.

As Oliver Wight principals are often heard asking, "What is the science behind your inventory policy?" One of the earliest examples of this we can recall was in the early 1990s when a marketing director was sketching something out on graph paper. He was a bit chuffed by the attention and the questioning and said, "Oh, I have all the product managers' forecasts, which are based on a couple of algorithms I've given them, and we're now comparing them with the actual results. I'm just eyeballing the variation to see how much safety stock we should hold." We suggested that there are algorithms that should be able to come up with a recommendation to save him time, but his response was, "Yes, I have a few in mind, but first I want my team to see it and understand what the graphs are telling them. For example, if they consistently underachieve their forecast, which most are doing at the moment, then we don't need safety stock. It is hard for a sales and marketing person to accept concepts like this, without first seeing it with their own eyes."

The "science" has obviously moved on since then, but the point of analyzing, removing *bias*, and seeing the impact still remains. In this case the marketing director was trying to assess what we call normal cause variation and set up stock to cover just that. There are other components to safety stock, such as lead times, shelf life, order quantities, distributed inventory, storage capability (such as cool room storage capacity), and customer expectations and contractual agreements, but the intent is the same. If we understand and cover the normal cause variation, the rest is just mechanical.

Often overlooked in the setting up of these buffers is the element of supply variation. We mentioned previously the *static data* used in the calculation, such as lead times and lot sizes, but there are environments, such as dairy, where milk volume and quality can vary considerably based on rainfall, the amount of sunshine, feed quality, and time of year. The same calculation, however, can be applied equally well to a material as a finished product. What is the variation, and what is needed to cover the variation, the lead time to replenish, and the minimum lot size? There are some who say we should be agile and be able to change and respond at a moment's notice, without incurring extra cost. We see being agile as an output of doing other things. For example, if we had a lead time of zero and a minimum lot size of one, then we could be infinitely agile. We will cover more on stocking policy and agility later in the book, but suffice it to say, if agility is your strategy, then the work needs to first start on reducing lead times, changeover times, and lot size across the supply chain.

Formal and consistently executed processes and clear roles and responsibilities are two areas that are linked and come from documenting what is done, and then refining and improving as we learn more. A manufacturing site we visited once had WIN posted up everywhere. It was written vertically and had in very small font alongside each letter: Write, It, Now. Apart from the fact that it had that winning emotion aroused, it applied to everything at that site. It referred to transaction timing, capturing error codes for root cause analysis, and defining ways of working and embedding the improvements.

Many organizations give lip service to this and then wonder why things go off track when someone leaves the organization. For consistent execution, processes need to be documented in policies and procedures, and then followed. Within this documentation, roles and responsibilities should be prominent. Then to close the loop, there needs to be a mechanism to routinely update the documentation to reflect current reality. Would you fly with an airline that allowed pilots to do their own thing and make it up as they went along? If lives depend on this level of process discipline and rigor in the airline industry, imagine how effective the supply planning and execution environment would be if that level of discipline was applied there, too.

Now that we have covered some of the key principles that we need to consider in supply execution, let's take a deeper dive and look at who is orchestrating these activities.

Master Planner/Scheduler as a Pivotal Role

Master is an important term in that the master plan or the master schedule then governs all other plans thereafter. We will discuss more on this later, but suffice it to say here that all other lower-level plans, such as the material, production, supplier, and capacity, are governed by this master plan or schedule. The role of master planner is usually associated with longer-range plans supporting the Integrated Business Planning process and, where applicable, encompasses all the nodes in that company's defined supply chain. The role in the Integrated Tactical Planning process is more likely to be associated with a supply point (as defined previously in the chapter), and the role is known as a master scheduler. Similar to other roles, it could be one role or a series of roles depending on size, complexity, and the structure of the organization and the design of the Integrated Tactical Planning matrix. In smaller companies, the two roles may be combined with the same person working to two different horizons, and in larger companies, it might be several people. The important point is that there is a clear time horizon in which the data go from an aggregate level of detail to a more granular level.

Terms have been evolving and many companies are replacing *master planner* and *master scheduler* with *supply planner* and *supply scheduler,* so to keep it simple, we'll refer to it from here on as *supply planner/ scheduler* as a cover all. The difference between the two roles is defined in Figure 5.3. The following are common planning systems terminology

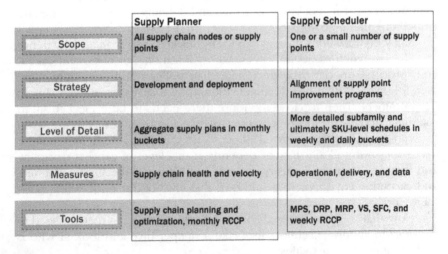

	Supply Planner	Supply Scheduler
Scope	All supply chain nodes or supply points	One or a small number of supply points
Strategy	Development and deployment	Alignment of supply point improvement programs
Level of Detail	Aggregate supply plans in monthly buckets	More detailed subfamily and ultimately SKU-level schedules in weekly and daily buckets
Measures	Supply chain health and velocity	Operational, delivery, and data
Tools	Supply chain planning and optimization, monthly RCCP	MPS, DRP, MRP, VS, SFC, and weekly RCCP

FIGURE 5.3 Supply Planner versus Supply Scheduler Roles

Source: Oliver Wight. Copyright Oliver Wight International, Inc. Used with permission.

we'll be referring to: master planning and scheduling (MPS); *distribution requirements planning (DRP)*; material requirements planning (MRP); vendor scheduling (VS); shop-floor control (SFC); rough-cut capacity planning (RCCP).

The supply planner/supply scheduler's role in Integrated Tactical Planning is to make sure the underlying drivers of planning are collated and accurate, for example, run rates, set-up times, lead times, and lot sizes for a specific site or subset of the whole supply chain. They analyze trends, such as demonstrated capacity; capture metrics, such as schedule adherence; and are involved in continuous improvement programs. They also play a key role in aligning plans and gaining agreement across the supply activities and facilitating the monthly supply point review (sometimes known as pre-*supply review* or site review), which feeds into the monthly Integrated Business Management process. In short, the supply planners/schedulers are the people with their fingers on the pulse and the go-to people if you want to know what is going on or what the latest issues are in relation to delivering the supply plan.

We often hear, "I create good plans; it is just that operations can't execute them!" To us, that just means we are not working cross-functionally as a team. Figure 5.4 shows all of the elements or people who contribute to a good plan, and the supply planner/scheduler needs to engage with all of these functions/roles. Just to make it clear: if plans are not being executed according to the plans, then we don't have a good plan. To truly create great plans, they must be realistic and doable. This means all functions align on, and agree to, the new plans each week, and then work together to make them happen thereafter.

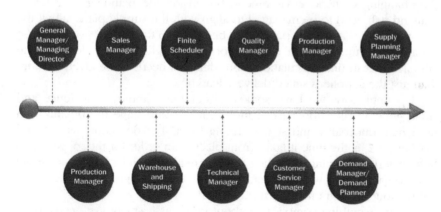

FIGURE 5.4 Who Else Is Involved

Source: Oliver Wight. Copyright Oliver Wight International, Inc. Used with permission.

Time Fence Management—The Next Level of Detail

Time fences were discussed in Chapters 2 and 4, but there is more depth to the planning time fence than just the cumulative lead time. The concept of the focus month is the time that the aggregate plans move inside the planning time fence and hence moves from an aggregate plan to a more detailed plan. The intent of this focus month is to zoom in on that month to ensure the transition is congruent from aggregate to detail and detail to aggregate. Remember, this is when the organization is starting to commit funds and apply resources to variable and semivariable costs. As a side note, the fixed part of the costs have already been signed off through the Integrated Business Planning cycle, possibly many months prior, and it is important to recognize that the Integrated Tactical Planning process is not a game of overhead recovery; its purpose is to stay on track to deliver the core plans as signed off in the latest Integrated Business Planning cycle, as well as the support plans, such as financial and inventory.

Inside the planning time fence, the Integrated Tactical Planning process team takes over the plans, knowing that they have been given the best possible set of plans from the Integrated Business Planning process. The reason we say that these plans are the best possible set of plans is that they should have been reviewed 20 or more times before the month in question enters the planning time fence. The intention then is to deliver the first 3 months of the signed-off plans, as well as manage the deployment of the contingencies to mitigate against vulnerabilities and leverage opportunities should they arise.

The primary change in behavior before and after the time fence is that, outside the planning time fence, the supply environment will flex to meet the changing demand environment, but inside the planning time fence, demand will need to be managed to align with the supply plans, albeit the assumption is that supply plans have been set up to manage normal cause variation. Figure 5.5 is an example of what might be considered in the cumulative lead time calculation. Consideration needs to be given to more than just the supplier's stated delivery lead time.

Up until now, we have spoken about the planning time fence and some general rules about calculation, but at some stage the organization must map out reality and start planning for it. The definition, as outlined in Chapter 2, is the time it takes from placing an order for the longest lead time material to having a finished product ready to sell or ship. In a supply chain environment, with no manufacturing, the principle is still the same, but without the extra manufacturing steps.

There is nothing complicated about it; the assessment just needs to be done. Sometimes when the analysis is done, the lead times are so long that the organization almost goes into denial and turns a blind eye to it. One

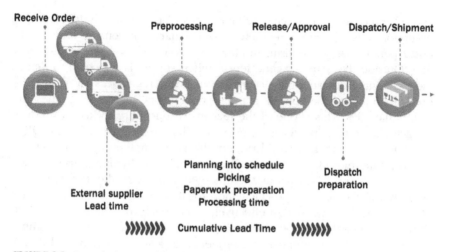

FIGURE 5.5 Cumulative Lead Time Calculation

Source: Oliver Wight. Copyright Oliver Wight International, Inc. Used with permission.

client even asked, "Customs has just doubled their inspection time from 2 weeks to 4 weeks; what do you think we should do?" The answer was simple, "Extend the planning time fence by 2 weeks." This is however, a blind spot that people can get into because as they went on to say, "But we have set up all our budgets and capacities for 2 weeks and this is going to wreck our plans!" That was true, but not as wrecked as they would be if they continued to plan with the current lead times, and everything ends up not only being 2 weeks late, but with an exponentially accumulating bow wave cascading forward in every plan as they constantly fail to play catch-up.

The other logical fallacy companies use is something called *effective lead time,* when they believe inventory is the answer. An example of this is when the suppliers manage the safety stock close to the site, so the lead time is just the time to draw off from the local storage location. The problem is that you can only consume this safety stock once, and then you're back to the real lead time, and if your supplier sources from a long way off, or has limited capacity, then this can cause significant disruption. The other issue is that MRP will not give you an alert because it is working to the shorter draw-off-location lead time and lot sizing.

The planning time fence is typically hardwired in the planning system, and most systems have this capability. The system then behaves differently inside the planning time fence to outside of it. Inside the planning time fence the system requires a person to make changes and will not make changes automatically, for example, firm an order, move an order, delete an order, and several other system-generated messages. The planning system will give exception messages any time there is an imbalance in demand and supply, but a person has to confirm, modify, or ignore the system recommendation. Outside the planning time fence, when supply is expected to flex to meet changing demand, the system automatically rebalances the plan without human input based on the planning parameters, such as lead times and order quantities. This is one of the reasons planners are so keen to reduce the actual planning time fence by using an effective time fence, because they see it as decreasing their workload, but this is yet another logical fallacy.

The time period that planners seem to be naturally drawn to is shown in Figure 5.6 and is known as the emergency zone, or the sold-out zone, as shown in Figure 5.7. The calculation for the emergency zone is defined as how long it takes to cost-effectively cycle back to a finished product, assuming material and labor are available. Typically manufacturing companies have an ideal manufacturing sequence of a week or two, and that is a good starting point to define the emergency zone. An example is a paint company sequencing production based on going from white to dark colors to minimize color contamination and to minimize changeover times through less time required for cleaning. Another company was set up to make certain products on certain days, which aided matching crew expertise with the type of product on their schedule.

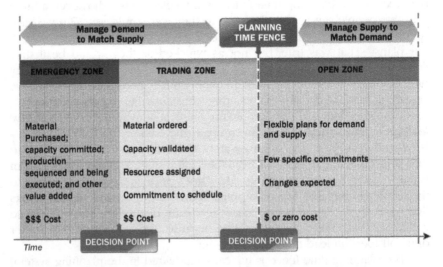

FIGURE 5.6 Emergency, Trading, and Open Zones in a Make-to-Stock Supply Environment

Source: Oliver Wight. Copyright Oliver Wight International, Inc. Used with permission.

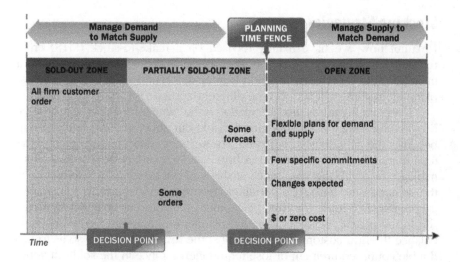

FIGURE 5.7 Make-to-Order Time Fences

Source: Oliver Wight. Copyright Oliver Wight International, Inc. Used with permission.

Changing in the emergency zone is very expensive and disruptive, and hence the goal is to have no or minimal changes inside this zone—as the name suggests, it has to be a justified emergency to change the schedule. Typically, this time fence is a process time fence and can't be hardwired into the system. Signing off the detailed plan inside the emergency zone is one of the critical agenda items for the Integrated Tactical Planning meeting and would follow a similar process as described in Chapter 2, Figure 2.7.

A planner once said during a somewhat heated discussion about time fences, "I'm only going to plan in the emergency zone, that is the next 2 weeks, because the computer can do the rest." When asked who was going to manage the supplier purchasing lead time, which was 12 weeks, there was a blank stare. He hadn't considered that all those changes in the trading zone and the noise he was experiencing was being created by his just-let-the-computer-do-it strategy. This also applies to using effective lead times. Anything outside that time ends up being out of sight, and out of mind for the planner and MRP . . . well, until there is a major shortage, and then all hell breaks loose.

We have heard some people say that they prefer to work in a supply chain environment where they don't need to worry about manufacturing, but what they lose in not having manufacturing to worry about is typically gained in increased lead times and the hidden manufacturing problems that their suppliers may face. It is usually easier to control what is inside your own four walls.

Stocking Strategies

Up until now, we have mainly focused on a make-to-stock (MTS) environment but there are other supply strategies to consider. For example, a make-to-order (MTO) environment is quite different from MTS but the most planning systems will support the different approaches.

The planning time fence calculation is the same for MTO as it is for MTS, but the emergency zone becomes the sold-out zone, and the trading zone becomes the partially sold-out zone. These zones relate to how much of the total demand has been realized in firm customer orders. Most systems can manage this, with the time fence at the sold-out zone often referred to as the demand time fence (but terminology varies across systems). This zone is composed of 100% confirmed customer orders and no residual forecast.

In the partially sold-out zone the planner and planning system need to balance the firm customer orders against the residual forecasts so as to not double count requirement or lose requirements. Once in the sold-out zone, however, customer orders are firm and cannot be changed . . . well, unless there is an emergency.

This leads to determining stocking strategy in support of the various approaches to the supply strategy. Like all things in life, there is one way of doing things, and then another, and another . . . but often the solution requires a hybrid approach. As we say at Oliver Wight, not all customers and SKUs are the same, and therefore not all stocking strategies should be the same. It must be aligned with customer and SKU importance, the cost to serve, and the route to market.

In Figure 5.8, the objective is to define the stocking strategy based on the overall supply model. There are whole books written on inventory policy and calculating the ideal level of inventory, but for the sake of brevity, these are the important questions to answer:

- Where do you want to meet the custom or position your products in the marketplace?
- What do our competitors do?
- How much does the proposed strategy cost?

This discussion is starting to touch on supply chain strategy and its inherent strengths and weaknesses, which is not the intent of this book. The important point here is to plan for what is now, not what might be hypothetically achieved in the future or requested through the budgeting process, and think beyond one individual node or supply point to consider the end-to-end picture.

Let's take a deeper dive into stocking strategy.

TO STOCK	HYBRID	TO ORDER
➢ Competitive lead time ➢ Manufacturing efficiency ➢ Manufacturing process constraint ➢ Seasonality ➢ Level employment	➢ Popular configurations ➢ Same item to stock and to order ➢ Build to semifinished product ➢ Strategic stocking (long lead times) ➢ Marketing versus manufacturing flexibility	➢ Cumulative lead time ➢ Inventory investment ➢ Capacity constraint ➢ Forecast variability ➢ Obsolescence

FIGURE 5.8 Supply Stocking Strategy

Source: Oliver Wight. Copyright Oliver Wight International, Inc. Used with permission.

Make to Order

Make to order means that finished goods are not available at the time the customer order is taken, but they will be available within a specified lead time as agreed with the customer. There are various types of make to order, with the three main ones being as described here:

- Finish to order

    This is almost a make-to-stock strategy, but the significant difference is that only a partially finished product is made and stocked in inventory, awaiting the final customer order to fully configure the product. For example, one of our clients wanted to move its barbeque manufacturing business to China, which was going to extend the lead time from 2 weeks to 12 weeks. Because customers expected the product to be either available in store, or, at least only a short wait, the extended lead time meant that they would lose flexibility to meet the sales pattern if it didn't go to forecast. Compounding that, 90% of the sales came in during the October/November/December period (southern hemisphere), in the lead-up to Christmas and the summer vacation. The solution was to use a finish-to-order supply strategy and leave the manufacture of the most difficult-to-forecast element of the barbeque—the colored lids and trim—with local production, and then finish the complete unit once the order was placed.

- Make to Order

    Make to order is when the product is manufactured only once the order is received. This means that cost is added only at the last minute, and the organization can be flexible in final configuration. However, to facilitate this, there still needs to be material, labor, and capacity available, which means that a forecast is still going to be required. The only difference is that the forecast is aligned at a lower level in the bills of materials, as well as the various options that the final order may request.

- Engineer to Order

Engineer to order is when the product is designed as part of the sales order process. For example, a client who made hydroelectrical systems for use in remote access water projects was dependent on the actual physical landscape as well as the amount of water involved to be able to do the final design. So, although many components of different installations were similar, each had to have specifications drawn and signed off before manufacturing. The advantages of this approach are that the cost to produce the item is covered in the order validation process, and there is no finished goods inventory to manage.

On a final note, there seems to be a general perception that the various strategies of make to order are harder to manage than a make-to-stock strategy, but we'd suggest that a make-to-stock strategy has its own difficulties, which we'll take a look at next.

Make to Stock

Make to stock means that finished goods are made ahead of customer orders and items are held in stock somewhere in the supply chain. In general, the intent is to shorten the lead time for the customer and gain a competitive advantage over those whose lead times and availability are less immediate. Other circumstances that would drive a make-to-stock strategy are short-shelf-life raw ingredients, such as in the dairy industry, when fresh milk is coming in every day and has to be converted into something within 36 hours. The finished goods then have an extended shelf life, ranging from 9 days for fresh milk to several months for cheeses and powdered milk.

Another example is Easter eggs, when demand is so great at Easter that it outstrips capacity and necessitates making Easter eggs all year round and stockpiling them in readiness.

A slight variation on a make-to-stock strategy is a make to forecast. This is when a customer has a unique finished goods requirement, and the company manufactures ahead of the customer order being placed. The advantage is that it reduces the order lead time for the customer, can be used to smooth capacity requirements, and can save on the cost of changeover times. The disadvantage is that if the customer does not order the product, it can not then be sold to anyone else—or at least the difficulty of doing so is high.

A make-to-stock strategy is much more dependent on a forecast than make to order and requires an understanding of where inventory will be held. For example, in an environment that has distributed inventory across many distribution supply nodes or distribution points, a form of forecast will be required at each distribution point for the end sale demand. Some might argue that the distribution point should just pull from the central warehouse or manufacturing location, which can work, but the caution is that we should not confuse an execution process with a planning process. The pull from a central location is an execution mechanism, and without any projected requirements and forward visibility, how can an effective plan be generated or an improvement program be assessed?

This does not mean a forecast is not required in a make-to-order environment. We may not react to a forecast of finished goods requirements directly, but there needs to be some projected requirements to ensure raw material and capacity are available in anticipation of sales orders, and these would be derived from the finished goods forecast. The rule of thumb is, if you can be competitive without having a finished product available at the time of receiving the sales order, then back up through the bill of material and set your supply strategy as far away from make to stock as possible.

The reasons are that once manufactured and in stock, those finished goods need to be managed, which incurs the cost of storage, counting, and protecting quality, not to mention the opportunity cost associated with conversion. It also reduces flexibility. Remember the barbeque manufacturer example we talked about? If they had continued with a fully finished goods import strategy, they would have been left with having to discount barbeques if the customer preference trend moved from, for example, enamel-colored trim to stainless steel during the season. What some of their more enlightened customers started doing was to buy a barbeque in winter when they knew they would get a really good price just to get rid of the excess inventory. Incidentally, that same company also sold wood-fired heaters, which if you bought in summer you could drive a bargain price.

As was discussed with the CEO at the time, just because the landed cost of the overseas-manufactured barbeques and wood-fired heaters were 15% lower does not necessarily mean you will make more money. With a "fashion" market and a forecast that needs to be very accurate at the 13-week horizon, margin will be eroded if demand is not there when the product arrives.

Decoupling Demand from Supply

The Integrated Tactical Planning process is largely about the trade-off between being infinitely flexible to meet all demands that arise and cost-effectively balancing demand with supply. The ultimate destination is to adopt a *takt time* approach, which, in simple terms, means that the rate of production is aligned with actual customer demand. To get to that level of alignment cost-effectively requires a level of continuous improvement to the stage in which the supply organization can do small and variable runs and change over from product to product in a short space of time, for example, in less than 10 minutes. Although it sounds simple, the journey to get there is far from straightforward and potential investment quite significant.

There are two forces operating here, as can be seen in Figure 5.9. There is the need for stability in production, at least while the organization climbs the continuous improvement curve, but also the inherent variability of demand. What needs to be in place is a formal and objective way of creating the buffers to protect against the variation and maintain the integrity of one set of integrated numbers. The first step is to set up the supply chain to at minimum meet of 95% of the time given normal cause variation.

There are several strategies for managing this:

- Carry safety stock, but not just any stock. Following on from what we discussed in the key aspects of supply execution, there needs to be an assessment of demand variation (there are various calculations, but one of the simpler approaches to get started with is to use the equation safety stock = customer service [e.g. 95% = 2.06 standard deviations] × mean absolute deviation [from the forecast] × lead time), by SKU and stocking location to cover lead times and meet the minimum expectations of customer delivery performance. Each one of these variables directly affects the level of required safety stock.
- Use the projected spare capacity to prebuild product, as long as the shelf life and storage capacities allow for the extra time the product

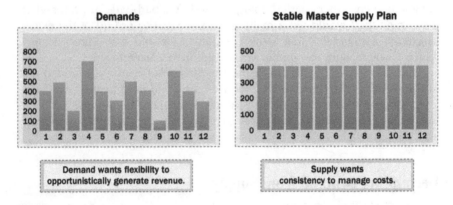

FIGURE 5.9 Master Supply Planning and Scheduling—The Conflict

Source: Oliver Wight. Copyright Oliver Wight International, Inc. Used with permission.

will be sitting in storage and the business can afford to tie up cash in holding this inventory.

- Build in safety capacity to the capacity planning process, and then through the weekly Integrated Tactical Planning process consume the capacity to match variability.
- Work toward matching capacity with the projected demand.
- Flex the lead time and align with future production runs and capability to produce through the available-to-promise function, which is part of most ERP systems' order-promising capability.
- Use lead time offsets to assist with bringing in materials and/or finished goods earlier.

It is important however to reinforce three key principles:

- The calculations need to have some science behind them—intuition in isolation is not a good guide to creating buffers.
- The inventory policy needs to be at a detailed level to align with demand variability, supply capability, storage, and shelf-life parameters. General and aggregate rules for buffers typically lead to more inventory *and* more stock outs.
- Try to have one mechanism for buffering in as smaller number of stocking points as practical—having multiple sites of safety and multiple calculations will only lead to confusion. As a planner said to us once, "Not only are the spreadsheets complicated and take a lot of manual work to regenerate each week, I've put so many buffers in there that now I can't remember where they all are!"

One strategy that we have left out because it is so important that it needs highlighting by exception is to be constantly working on reducing demand bias and variability. There is evidence to show that a 30% improvement in forecast accuracy leads to a 15% decrease in inventory, and if bias is eliminated in the forecast, then in the safety stock calculations, lead time can be substituted with cycle time, which has been demonstrated to dramatically decrease buffer stock *and* increase customer delivery performance.

Ultimately, better demand planning and demand execution are the most cost-effective ways to take uncertainty out of the business. We are not saying it will completely remove uncertainty or unforeseen events, but taking an incremental approach will reduce the costly need for buffers.

In summing up, our recommendation is to plan to the current circumstances, determine what is needed to meet variability in customer requirements *and* achieve smooth production. While this is happening, the continuous improvement program needs to be driving toward the ideal takt time alignment.

Demonstrated Capacity Planning

Demonstrated capacity was discussed as an overview concept in Chapter 1, and here we are going to dive into a little more detail, with specific reference to supply capability. Capacity refers to the capability of items to move through a work center in a given time period. Most companies refer to a machine or manufacturing line capability, but the definition is much broader. It not only considers production capability but could also include warehouse capacity, skilled labor output, and even a supplier's capability. For one of our pharmaceutical clients, one of the bottleneck work areas was the quality department's inspection time, which was consistently taking a week longer than estimated in the routings.

The first step is to understand the demand requirements and the *required capacity* needed to support those plans. This is often referred to as "assuming infinite capacity", and is important in that it can then be matched back to actual capability to highlight the areas of mismatch. If the assumption of finite capacity is used initially, then opportunities to smooth plans, stretch a little on shifts, optimize, and prioritize will be lost because finite capacity hides problems before they are identified.

The second step is to match required capacity against demonstrated capacity, which reflects what each work center has demonstrated it is capable of in the recent past, for example, during the last 6 weeks. This is the valid capacity of what each work center can do under the current conditions, considering product mix, shift patterns, staff levels, efficiency, and utilization.

Demonstrated capacity, however, is not an absolute guide to future capability. Changes can be made by adding a shift or extra machines, improving throughput, or using third-party providers. There are also things that can detract from throughput, such as machine deterioration, new people being less skilled, and the uncertainty of producing new products to specification and on time.

So, past performance is just one input into deriving demonstrated capacity. It needs a formal process to measure actual performance, analyze those actuals to remove outliers, and take input from the work center supervisor to adjust for anticipated changes (decreases as well as increases). This becomes the commitment that each work center will produce in the future.

The result is planned (demonstrated) capability, which is expected to be available during a specific future time period. It is based on the demonstrated capacity but adjusted by any changes expected by the work center supervisor. This may mean adding or deleting shifts, people, machines, overtime, or productivity improvements.

The maximum (demonstrated) capacity establishes a higher level of capacity that could be accomplished if a supervisor were to work the maximum overtime, add a shift, or hire people to run all the equipment in parallel. It is the maximum amount a work center can produce without capital expenditure for equipment or facilities. Typically, maximum capacity is not sustainable over a longer period of time but can be used to manage peak requirements. Figure 5.10 is an example of a time-phased capacity planning graphic, required capacity by product, planned (demonstrated) capacity, and maximum capacity.

The next step is to identify critical work areas. Modeling every area of required capacity could be very time-consuming and unnecessary. In most organizations there are only a few work areas that are constrained or critical. These might just be slower than the upstream or downstream work areas; they may be bottlenecks, such as one packer for several manufacturing lines; or they may just be expensive if overloaded, such as renting extra refrigerated storage space. As a rule of thumb, we would recommend modeling only the critical work areas, not usually more than six, with the assumption that if they are being well managed, the rest of the work areas around them will flow smoothly. One other area that may be added to the modeling is underused work areas. One of our clients was doing such good job of improving inventory management in one of their warehouses, it modeled their overflow warehouse to be able to assess when it might be feasible to stop using it and save money on rent and labor.

There are some great references to capacity planning, such as *Gaining Control* (Correll & Herbert, 2007), so more detailed information can be found in that text, but to draw this section back to the Integrated Tactical Planning process, rough-cut capacity planning is a key input into the monthly Integrated Business Planning process, and when the plan comes into the planning time fence, weekly rough-cut capacity planning is used and usually converted from a resource profile at the aggregate level to a more detailed level, such as a SKU-based *load profile*, to view in the Integrated Tactical Planning meeting. This is sometimes known as rough-cut capacity planning type II.

Inventory Management

This leads to another set of guidelines that the Integrated Tactical Planning process will keep a pulse check on, and that is inventory policy. Inventory in most organizations is a constant struggle to keep under control. Often in organizations we see inventory issues ranging from too much, to too little,

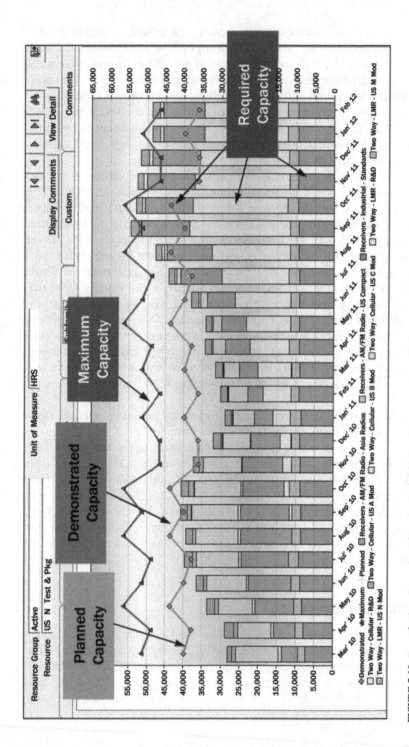

FIGURE 5.10 Rough-Cut Capacity Planning Simulation

Source: Oliver Wight. Copyright Oliver Wight International, Inc. Used with permission.

or to too much of the wrong stock, in the wrong place, at the wrong time. This can stem from these reasons:

- Inventory management is governed by general rules.
- Similarly, but worth noting further, the policy is not to a sufficient level of detail, that is, by SKU.
- The frequency of review is insufficient to keep up with changing circumstances.
- Inventory is seen as something that can be managed directly, instead of as an output from other process, for example, the quality of demand and supply plans.
- There is inefficient use of the planning tools/modules, such as master production scheduling.

As Figure 5.11 shows, inventory can be composed of legitimate parts and then some unknowns.

Inventory policy is insufficient in its title. When most businesspeople hear the term *inventory policy,* they automatically think safety stock and finished goods, and "It's a supply chain thing." Inventory policy is much broader than just safety stock. It should be a detailed policy that covers these issues:

- Finished goods, raw and packaging materials, intermediates, and distributed inventory.
- Use and supply strategy classification, for example, A, B, and C, as well as the D-for-delete criteria.
- Lead time, cycle time, manufacturing sequencing, and storage and shelf-life considerations.

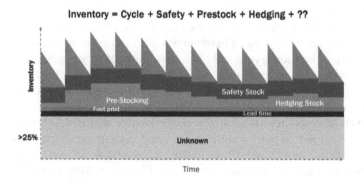

Inventory = Cycle + Safety + Prestock + Hedging + ??

FIGURE 5.11 Inventory Management

Source: Oliver Wight. Copyright Oliver Wight International, Inc. Used with permission.

- Lot sizing for manufacturing and customer ordering and minimum order quantities from suppliers.
- Finally, there needs to be an ability to value the policy (a simple and effective value calculation is [½ lot size + safety stock], and if there are rules allowing some consumption of safety stock without first seeking authority, which there should be, a slightly expanded calculation is [½ lot size + safety stock] − [½ the agreed consumption of safety before evoking the allocation policy]).

Once the inventory policy is in place, there should be no unknowns, as shown in Figure 5.11. It should be a deliberate assessment of the stocking points, manufacturing and supplier capability, the need to be competitive, and a detailed review of everything that is held currently to understand and agree why it is needed. It seems like common sense, but it is worth noting here that some logical fallacies we routinely hear from companies are about inventory planning and management.

Common Fallacies

Monthly planning is good enough for us. The issue with monthly planning is that the planning system will stack up all the requirements at the end of the previous month, not only for finished goods, but all the materials and consumption of capacity so that you have everything you need for the month ready on day 1. If, however, we cut requirements into weekly buckets and manufacture more often, then inventory will be potentially cut by a factor of four, which MRP will drive by staging the requirements through the month.

A client once said, "But we only take one order a month from our customers and they are happy with us to deliver anytime in the month, so therefore we only have to make it once a month." The lightbulb went on, however, with our reply, which was, "Even so, could we manage customer orders to stagger the week of manufacture and shipment to smooth requirements across the month *and* still meet customer delivery expectations? Also, if we said to our customers that we could help them reduce the cost of their working capital by delivering weekly instead of monthly, do you think they would be interested?"

Inventory policy is a supply chain responsibility. Although inventory management is part of supply chain and operations' responsibility, the actual policy is not. Think about the logic behind it: sales and marketing are interested in it for product availability. Finance is interested because of the cost of working capital. Warehousing is interested because of storage and picking capability. Operations is interested because they have to make products. Finally supply chain is interested because they are managing cost and delivery performance. Therefore, there is only one person who is ultimately accountable for inventory policy, and that is the CEO, supported by the lead team.

Larger lot sizes, longer customer lead times, and more safety stock will better cover capacity issues. This is another one we hear often, and it indicates that there is a general misunderstanding of how planning works. Think about it this way: each time we increase one of those parameters, it is consuming time that we could be making something else. If you are in a supply chain environment with no manufacturing, the same thing happens; it just shifts the burden more heavily on storage capability. Either way, it ends up decreasing flexibility and increasing costs. However, if we were to cut the lot sizes down to half and make them (or order them twice as often), cycle stock is effectively halved, and flexibility is doubled.

So why isn't this just common sense and everyone looks at small runs more often? There is usually one hurdle that gets in the way and that is changeover and start-up times. Logically, therefore, that means the focus must be put into reducing changeover times, not increasing run lengths. There are also other areas that affect this, and they are supplier minimum order sizes, the physical nature of the equipment such as vessel size, and, sometimes, as we had with one medical device company, the actual time to make one part end to end could be several weeks. The point is to keep asking the question, "How can we reduce lead times and lots sizes?" As we often say, "Absolute flexibility and agility will come only from having a lead time of zero and a lot size of one; so, ultimately, it becomes a never-ending journey of improvement."

You can only get 99+% customer delivery performance with more inventory. For this exercise, we are going to draw on the safety stock calculation—customer service requirement × lead time × forecast error— we discussed previously in this chapter. Although the customer delivery performance expectations in this calculation will drive more inventory, it is important to keep in mind that inventory policy should be at a line level and not a set of general rules.

If we bring in a different way of thinking and use the Pareto principle, we can optimize both inventory and customer delivery performance. Here is how. The following table is a summary of the thinking.

Item	% Value/ Volume	% of SKU	Demand Accuracy	Supply Frequency	Forward Cover Requirements	Impact on Inventory	Management Strategy
A SKUs	80	20	High	High	Low	High	Focus on the vital few
B SKUs	15	30	Medium	Medium	Medium	Medium	Some focus
C SKUs	5	50	Low	Low	High	Low	Set and forget

The logic is that A SKUs usually have inherent characteristics that help reduce the impact on overall inventory. As the table shows, there are only a few of them, but they are bigger, and their overall forecast accuracy is likely to be relatively higher because of the law of large numbers. Also, because they are bigger, they can be made more often and in relatively smaller lot sizes in comparison to the overall sales volume, which in turn increases supply frequency and the need for less forward cover.

If we also focus more intently on those items to remove bias from the forecast, cycle time to come back and manufacture the product again can be used in the safety stock calculation, instead of the total cumulative lead time. In typical organizations, lead times can be somewhere from 8 to 13 weeks, but cycle time is generally no more than 2 or 3 weeks. Covering a 2-week cycle time instead of a 13-week lead time takes a serious chunk out of the safety stock calculation. Also, if you think this doesn't apply to a supply chain business, then think again. Imagine you could reduce the lead time component of the calculation to the replenishment cycle; for example, if you get deliveries every week, then a week is used in the calculation instead of 13 weeks? It would have a huge impact.

The B SKUs sit somewhere in between the A and C strategies, but for the extreme argument, C SKUs are a nuisance on many fronts. They are tiny in value and volume, they tend to have poor forecast accuracy because of the law of small numbers, and their supply frequency is usually long. They tend to need more forward cover, but overall, that impact on inventory is small. So, the management strategy should be to work out how to set and forget the C SKUs until they are deleted or turn them into stars. The logical fallacy for A SKUs is to hold more safety stock, because they are important, but we'd recommend that we reverse the thinking and hold more safety stock of the C SKUs because they are not important but cause a lot of noise and disruption. Remember, the Pareto principle estimates that they are only 5% of the SKU volume, so doubling safety stock is still only a tiny impact. If you doubled safety stock for an A SKU, then that would have a massive impact.

The Right Level of Detail for Master Planning and Scheduling

Oliver Wight was a great fan of the term *roughly right,* and with the dynamic nature of the world we live in, it is as true today as it ever was. There is a point in time, however, that detailed plans are needed. For the Integrated Business Planning process where the focus is 24+ months, product aggregates (often referred to as *families*) should be all that is needed. One company we worked with did have a SKU view for their Integrated Business Planning process, but that SKU was just one super A SKU, worth 30% of the value of the SKU range. It was for all intents and purposes, a family all by itself. The point to make is that in most circumstances an aggregate view is all that is required for the medium to long term.

As a mental exercise, and to reinforce the point, we had one client who insisted on looking at every SKU, by week, out to a modest horizon of 12 months. Although that sounds doable and reasonable, think of it this way:

Number of SKUs = 1, 800

Number of periods = 52

Number of data sets = 4 (last year, this week, last week, and budget)

Therefore, the number of data points to manage is 1,800 × 52 × 4 = 374,400!

How do you manage that every week? The simple answer is that you don't!

The objective then is to look at different levels of detail over different horizons and only have the detail when it is absolutely required.

In the longer term, as mentioned previously in the chapter under Demonstrated Capacity, the supply plan for the Integrated Business Planning process would use rough-cut capacity planning to view the aggregate (family) load on the business by month, by critical work area, out to the 24+ month horizon. This is sometimes referred to as rough-cut capacity planning type I, which is at an aggregate level and in monthly time frames.

As we come into the Integrated Tactical Planning horizon, the plan needs to be cut down into weeks and matched against the weekly phasing

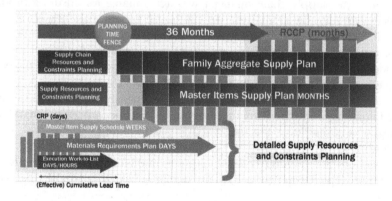

FIGURE 5.12 Month-Weekly-Daily for Capacity

Source: Oliver Wight. Copyright Oliver Wight International, Inc. Used with permission.

derived from the disaggregated demand plan that we discussed in Chapter 4. This is also tested against critical work areas, but using rough-cut capacity planning type II, which means the plan is at a detailed level, such as by SKU and by critical work area, the plan will highlight the impact of any change in mix of SKUs going through that work area. Remember, this is at least 13 weeks out, so there is still time to smooth out requirements in the trading zone before it moves into the emergency zone.

Then, in the really short term, when plans are going to move into the emergency zone, the plan will need to go down to the lowest level of detail and is often driven by *capacity requirements planning (CRP)*, which is typically by day or by shift, and balanced against queue levels preceding the work center and the flow downstream thereafter. Not all organizations need that level of detail in capacity planning, and many do just fine with a dispatch list from the master schedule. The important point is that there needs to be an ability to flow from aggregate plans to detail plans seamlessly across the planning time fence and then across the emergency time fence.

Aligning the Supply Chain

At the heart of aligning the supply chain is Oliver Wight's Universal Equation, which takes the *independent demand* requirements and uses that one set of numbers to flow from customer requirements; through distribution, manufacturing, materials requirements, capacity planning; and then out to supplier requirements. The issue we see often, however, is that there is a role defined as supply chain manager, but responsibilities, processes, and technology do not support the supply chain role. For example, in one retail business, the supply chain manager was accountable for ensuring product was delivered to the store from the warehouse greater than 98% of the time in full, but she was frustrated by breaks in the process and system. The forecast was not shared with her, the buyers managed all supplier orders and products, and the spreadsheet planning system only looked out for 6 weeks, even though the average supplier lead time was 12 weeks.

Although supply chain planning is more usually represented through the Integrated Business Planning process, if it has been poorly defined and integrated at that level, the Integrated Tactical Planning process will suffer accordingly.

So how do we address this in an Integrated Tactical Planning process sense? As depicted in Figure 5.13, the equation asks four simple questions:

1. What do we need?
2. When do we need it?
3. How much do we already have?
4. What more do I need to order and when?

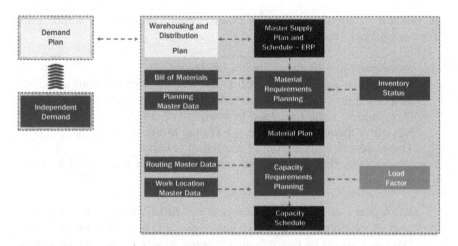

FIGURE 5.13 Oliver Wight's Universal Equation Covering the Nodes in the Immediate Supply Chain

Source: Oliver Wight. Copyright Oliver Wight International, Inc. Used with permission.

The questions are simple, but the execution can be difficult if it is done by manual systems and spreadsheets. It is important to emphasize that this is what an MRP planning system is meant to do and can do in seconds what a human being might do in hours or days. It just needs to be set up appropriately.

MRP is a modeling tool and at its heart it is just a great big calculator that is dependent on the setup parameters to calculate correctly. Translate that statement as accurate data and planning parameters that reflect reality. This is the second point to emphasize, which is that an MRP planning system is meant to simulate reality—it's not hypothetical, it's not built on aspirational results, and it's not built on banking all the continuous improvement initiatives before they are demonstrated—it's real and valid as we know the environment to be today.

If this is understood and applied, then we have the beginnings of effectively and seamlessly joining up the first-tier customers and first-tier suppliers through one set of integrated numbers, which can be checked for alignment weekly through the Integrated Tactical Planning process.

The important point is that independent demand coming from the first-tier customers then becomes *dependent demand* through the rest of the supply chain, all the way to the vendor schedules shared with the first-tier suppliers. All the requirements must be included in the independent demand plan for this demand picture to be complete and should, as closely as possible, resemble reality. This sounds simple, but here are some examples of breaks in the data set:

- Spare parts requirements are not integrated.
- Weekly phasing is not reflected in the weekly demand plans.
- Scheduled downtime is not included in the supply schedule.
- New product trials are added in as an afterthought.
- Not every manufacturing step is reflected in the routings.
- There are materials left out of the bill of material.
- Vendors are excluded from seeing future requirements until an order is placed.

Missing any of these considerations will cause manual intervention at best and chaotic planning at worst. Either way it is a costly exercise.

Even in a world of increasingly complex supply chains, which can be characterized by an array of in-house manufacturing, third-party manufacturing or product value-add activity, and purchased-in finished goods, supply chains **have to be mapped**, understood, and planned and managed as a whole. Figure 5.14 is an example of a relatively simple supply chain schematic of the material flow. Although this is a relatively simple example, of multiple products and materials, in-bound and out-bound transport lanes, and inter-site transfers are included, it can become complex. Mapping it and visualizing it can unlock a wealth of opportunities.

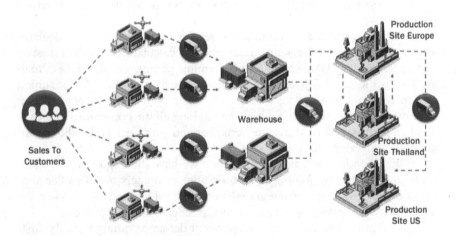

FIGURE 5.14 Inter-Site Supply Chain Model

Source: Oliver Wight. Copyright Oliver Wight International, Inc. Used with permission.

As discussed in Chapter 1, an essential activity is to map out the supply chain and define each *node* in terms of roles and behaviors, process integrity, use of technology, policies, and metrics.

The second step is to structure the management of the supply chain and the structure of the Integrated Tactical Planning process to mimic how it works today. We will talk more about it in Chapter 7, but because Integrated Tactical Planning is a more detailed process than Integrated Business Planning, there may be a need for more than one Integrated Tactical Planning process.

The third step is to plan for improvement. Once the thinking and management switches from supply points to supply chain, it elevates the need to understand and work to time fences that span that supply chain, as Figure 5.15 depicts.

The end-to-end cumulative lead time then becomes more important than the single entity. Each entity's emergency and trading zones should be mapped out and a supply chain strategy agreed to optimize the whole. For example, calculating safety stock then becomes a supply chain strategy, not a site strategy. The simple rule is that the supply chain holds buffers only in one place. In an MTS environment, this is typically as close to the final consumer as possible. This is, however, a hypothetic position, and in less mature supply chains there needs to be time allowed to migrate to this ideal state. In supply chains that have long lead times, the agreement is often to

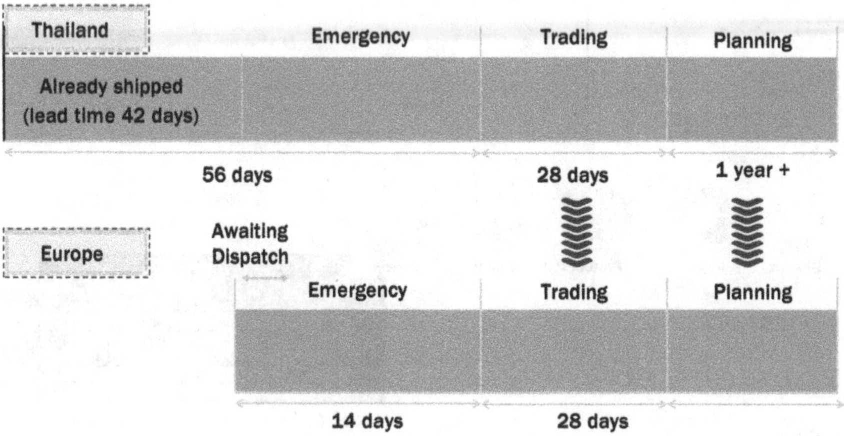

FIGURE 5.15 Example Time Fences

Source: Oliver Wight. Copyright Oliver Wight International, Inc. Used with permission.

hold safety stock close to the consumer *and* close to the most upstream supply chain node. Whatever strategy is pursued, it is important that there is a plan to collaborate on where and what is held as buffers.

To close the loop on the first-tier to first-tier supply chain, purchasing often gets left out, and it is unfathomable as to why in this age of fast and sophisticated technologies that purchasing is still raising purchase requisitions for MRP items, getting approvals to spend, and planning in spreadsheets, not to mention the inordinate amount of time spent chasing down deliveries. As Figure 5.15 shows, this is just a waste of time. If, however, we get the independent demand through the master supply plan, driving all other plans, then the next logical step is to extend out to our key suppliers with vendor schedules. A more expansive dive into supplier management and development programs can be found in *Purchasing in the 21st Century* (Schorr, 1998).

The benefits of sharing information and aligning on a seamless ordering process is shown in Figure 5.16. The traditional approach has many steps, from raising a purchase requisition, right though to delivery of product, which is clumsy and time-consuming. By using the one set of numbers concept and communicating with key suppliers through vendor scheduling straight out of the system, an enormous amount of time and effort can be eliminated.

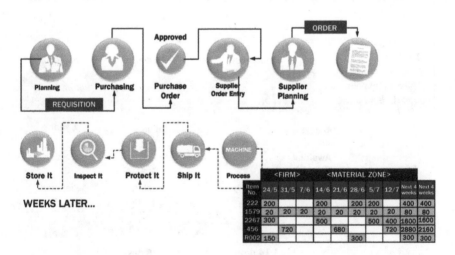

FIGURE 5.16 Purchase Order Lead Time

Source: Oliver Wight. Copyright Oliver Wight International, Inc. Used with permission.

To make it work, however, the organization needs to apply the same rules to our supply chain partners as we have recommended for the internal organization. Also note that if the organization does not have this level of discipline applied internally, then don't even start doing this with your suppliers. Once it is in place, then the following will need to be ensured to create an effective and trusting relationship:

- Agreed definitions of time fences and managing changes to plans.
- Having supplier visibility of requirements as far out as they need to plan cost effectively.
- Sharing plans from the system so that the manual work such as placing orders and following up deliveries is eliminated.
- Having planning based on agreed parameters, such as lead times, lot sizes, quality specifications, and price.

Both parties can assist each other with continuous improvement and agree to share the benefits when realized.

We often get push back on this, with procurement saying something like, "We can't do this for all our suppliers—we'd end up with chaos!" and that is probably true. What we can do is to segment our supplier base using a set of criteria that rank those that we want a strong and close relationship with and those items that are better purchased through spot buys and commodity markets. The important point to keep in mind is that every supplier included in this approach will proportionately reduce wasted time and unnecessary administration.

What then makes it into the Integrated Tactical Planning process are the exceptions to the material and supplier plans.

To circle back to data—just to reinforce the importance of that information—we would like to close out this chapter with some final words. We have spent a lot of time on the planning and integration aspects of effectively managing supply and supply chains, but none of this is going to work if the data in the system are questionable. There are key data elements that the Integrated Tactical Planning process would naturally include, such as inventory record accuracy, planning parameters, capacity profiles, and time fence management, as depicted in Figure 5.17.

The challenge for many organizations, however, is proactively managing data. When we ask clients how accurate their key data masters are, they usually say, "Great!," but when our response is, "How do you know?" we usually hear something like, "Well, um, arh . . . I only have to make a couple of adjustments each week, and so it must be OK."

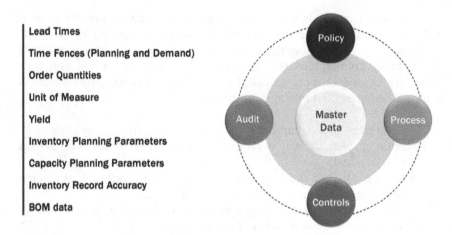

Lead Times

Time Fences (Planning and Demand)

Order Quantities

Unit of Measure

Yield

Inventory Planning Parameters

Capacity Planning Parameters

Inventory Record Accuracy

BOM data

FIGURE 5.17   System Capability Is Dependent on Data Integrity

Source: Oliver Wight. Copyright Oliver Wight International, Inc. Used with permission.

This raises two issues:

- How much time is spent retrospectively fixing those errors, and how much noise does it create for others?
- What seems like only a small thing to a supply planner, for example, if it is also happening to purchasing, material handlers, warehouse, quality, pricing, and any other users of the planning system, there is a cumulative effect that creates a massive problem and is usually the single most common reason we have heard for not using the planning system and opting for spreadsheets.

This is more than just data accuracy; as mentioned earlier, having a proactive approach to keeping the data as clean as possible requires *policy and procedures*, discipline in following plan change protocols, and an ongoing induction program to make sure anyone new to business understands how important accurate data are to the business.

Summary and Key Change Requirements

In this chapter we have covered the key elements of supply planning and execution as it relates to Integrated Tactical Planning . . . and a bit more. The point is that supply scheduling and execution should be part of supply chain thinking rather than the more myopic supply point thinking.

A key player in the process is the master supply planner/scheduler, who is responsible for representing all the supply plans, the integrity of the supply planning processes, and integrating plans from independent demand right through to the same data driving manufacturing and purchasing. An important time fence is the planning time fence that signals the need to prorate the aggregate Integrated Business Planning process plans into a more granular level and into weekly time periods, usually using rough-cut capacity planning type II to test validity out beyond the next few weeks. At the emergency change time fence, the detail is usually by SKU, key work center, by day, often using detailed CRP.

Mapping out the supply chain and understanding its current performance and potential for improvement is critical. It is primarily a strategic activity and although it should be managed through the Integrated Business Planning process, the detailed execution parts of those plans will play an important role in the Integrated Tactical Planning process.

It is vital that demonstrated capability is used as the fundamental driver of supply plans. This is critical in creating valid and doable plans. It is also highly recommended that there is a stated strategic intent to eliminate data holding and planning spreadsheets and optimize the use of the ERP planning system modules as the only source of truth.

Finally, none of this can work effectively without high levels of data accuracy. Master data files need to have a formal, rigorous, and proactive approach to make sure whatever is in the system is used and trusted.

If we bring this all together through the cross-functional Integrated Tactical Planning process, the supply chain can be effectively leveraged as a competitive advantage.

The following areas of change are typically required:

PEOPLE AND BEHAVIOR CHANGES
- One of the four key roles needed to form the quorum is the supply planner/scheduler.
- Adherence to time fences is not only critical for a supply chain node but also for the whole supply chain, including understanding our suppliers' capability.
- Understanding that not all SKUs and customers are equal with supply planning and management is often a difficult pill to swallow.
- Valid plans come from using demonstrated capability—banking more too early is a recipe for disaster.

PROCESS CHANGES
- Supply planning depends on a weekly cadence; monthly just does not cut it.

- The weekly cadence is critical for picking up changes and replanning to stay on track to the latest signed-off Integrated Business Planning set of plans.
- Definitions of appropriate time fences are critical for managing changes to supply plans.
- The supply plan is more than finished goods; the master schedule drives all lower-level plans with an integrated and single set of numbers.
- A formal and routine demonstrated capacity planning process is fundamental to creating valid plans.

TECHNOLOGY CHANGES

- Use the planning system, not spreadsheets, to generate one set of integrated plans that aligns plans from demand planning and order entry right through to vendor schedules.
- Integrity of the master data is the number one priority if the information is inaccurate.
- Use work center information for capacity planning.
- Simulation capability is essential for modeling and assessing multiple futures.

CHAPTER 6

Driving Performance Improvement
The Management Agenda: Too Busy to Improve?

O ne of the common symptoms that we see when working with clients on improving the effectiveness of their planning and execution in the Integrated Tactical Planning zone is the too-busy-to-improve syndrome. As we identified in the Introduction it often feels like everyone is running around putting out the latest fire, only to look up and run into, what appears on the surface, another isolated one-off incident, another fire to put out. This cycle continues and becomes for those who are working within it like being a hamster stuck on a hamster wheel, just trying to keep up with the issues that keep coming (see Figure 6.1). The result is that too often those involved feel helpless, frustrated, and in the worst cases experience personal burnout as "things never seem to get any better around here."

The whole premise of Integrated Tactical Planning is that great results come from great execution. No business that we have worked with has stated that their ambition is to have low service levels to their customers, to be writing off millions of dollars of obsolete inventory each year, to be spending hundreds of thousands of dollars on premium freight and overtime, or incurring the cost of absenteeism or recruitment resulting from stressed and poorly engaged employees. However, that is the reality for many organizations in which short-term planning and execution are poor.

Depending on the performance of other companies in the market segments and channels in which the business competes, great or excellent execution will at worst provide the foundation performance to enable the company to play in the market and at best will provide competitive advantage for the company as performance differentiates against peers. Irrespective of which situation describes the reality for your organization, great execution will reduce the amount of noise and result in lower costs in multiple areas.

FIGURE 6.1 The Execution Hamster Wheel

So, if the agenda is to improve execution and thus drive performance improvement, while also freeing employees from the execution hamster wheel, it is essential to deliberately create time for employees to spend on improvement and to design this into your Integrated Tactical Planning process. But how do you know where to focus your improvement efforts?

Measures: Powerful Tools for Improvement but . . .

In the preceding chapters we have already identified a number of measures that the team involved in Integrated Tactical Planning should be considering. But before we look at those in more detail let us get clear on why measurement is important and what are some of the pitfalls to look out for.

Why Measure?

The question "Why measure?" seems like an odd one to ask because in most companies measures are everywhere. In most businesses that we work with we see organizations that are overrun with measures. Key performance indicators (KPIs) and sometimes key KPIs abound, along with dashboards and KPI reporting decks.

Unfortunately, all too often we see people spending an inordinate amount of time compiling data and reporting the latest results, with the effort outweighing the benefit. Following are some symptoms of environments like this:

- Too many measures, making it difficult for managers to understand where they should focus.
- Out-of-date measures or infrequently updated measures.
- Measures reviewed and discussed in multiple meetings that do not appear to be owned by anyone.
- Measures that drive conflict within the organization.
- Measures with no targets.
- Measures defined with the sole purpose of showing "good" performance.
- Nothing being done to address measures in which targets are routinely not be achieved.

So, to understand why organizations who are exhibiting these symptoms are not achieving the return on effort, let's first have a look at the purpose of measures. As Dick Ling and Walt Goddard called out when they first described S&OP in their book *Orchestrating Success* (1988, p. 100), "Performance measurements are not ends in themselves; rather, they are used to take the pulse of the business and catch problems before they become crises. Moreover, by reviewing performance, you should be able to uncover the underlying causes of difficulties and find appropriate remedies."

Measuring performance provides essential feedback that enables two fundamental elements of Integrated Tactical Planning:

- Monitoring and control.
- Improvement.

MONITORING AND CONTROL As we discussed in Chapter 1, a symptom that many companies report in the tactical planning and execution zone is lack of control. Using measures to monitor progress against the execution plan and to indicate when control is being lost is a prerequisite to taking back control. The technique of demand monitoring, shared in Chapter 4, is an example of this. In this case, weekly demand plan consumption is monitored and tolerances or control limits used to trigger actions to get back in control and/or escalate the issue in the instance when tolerances are exceeded.

The following outlines the four elements of measuring for control:

- **An output to measure**—in the case just described, actual sales.
- **A standard against which to compare**—in the case just described, the weekly demand plan.

- **A tolerance**—to allow for normal variation or process capability and hence define the trigger points for action; in the case just described, set as a + or − % variation to the weekly demand plan.
- **Corrective action**—actions or rules for how to respond if the measure exceeds the tolerance; in the case just described, actions could include increasing or decreasing the demand plan, conducting *root cause analysis* and making decisions on adjusting the subsequent weeks' demand plans, or taking additional action to stimulate demand to get back on track or to constrain demand to match to any supply constraint.

IMPROVEMENT   Measures are the vital first step in exposing process performance problems but only if they are correctly defined and you do something with them. As depicted in Figure 6.2, the measurement needs to be reported, the root cause of any nonperformance determined, action needs to be taken to address the root cause and thus improve the problem, and then the impact of those actions needs to be understood when subsequent measurement is undertaken; and so the cycle goes on.

The But . . . Measurement Pitfalls to Avoid. Although the positive impact on a business of measures that are used for control and improvement can be huge, there are a number of negative outcomes that the injudicious use of measures can create.

> **You cannot fatten the pig by weighing it.** Unless you do something with the measure, that is, use it to monitor and control or use it to drive improvement, then it is a waste. When I visit companies that show me dashboards of measures proudly displayed on walls or screens that, after prompting, are revealed to be used for neither control nor improvement, my reaction is to suggest replacing the dashboard with a picture of some flowers or a landscape . . . it looks nicer and you only have to pay for it once, unlike measures that are typically collected, calculated, displayed, and reported regardless of whether you do something with them or not.

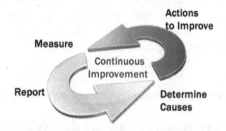

FIGURE 6.2 The Improvement Process

Source: Oliver Wight. Copyright Oliver Wight International, Inc. Used with permission.

Too many measures. The *K* stands for key for a reason. We often work with organizations that suffer from measure overload, and similar to trying to fatten the pig by weighing it, they end up doing nothing with the measures because they have too many to effectively handle. The use of the term key performance indicator has been adopted to describe every measurement in some organizations, who then go on to talk about their "key" KPIs. Such an environment is often symptomatic of a lack of an integrated view into the business about which processes are essential to deliver on the organizational goals, and thus which are the "key" things to measure.

Measures and targets drive behavior—use them wisely. We have observed KPIs driving undesirable outcomes, such as these examples:

- Seeing an employee who was writhing in pain on the floor of a staff locker room, suffering an appendicitis, being abused and then ignored by his colleagues who thought that he had incurred a work injury that would cost them their safety performance–related bonus.
- Employees passing through out-of-specification parts to a downstream production process so that they could break a production record and win the prize of a company baseball cap and their name up in lights on the notice board.

Measures driving conflict. Measures at a functional or departmental level that are misaligned can be a major source of internal organizational and personal conflict. A personal experience of one of the authors is recounted in this story: This experience occurred early in my career when I was in the role of operations manager and found myself standing toe-to-toe in the car park of my workplace having a very robust conversation with the sales and marketing manager, who was expressing his view in no uncertain terms that I was undermining his efforts. We did not come to blows but the volume and passion of our conversation was sufficient to bring a significant number of the production team out from the canteen during their lunch break to spectate. The root cause of our heated conversation was that I was being measured on factory efficiency and utilization. My sales and marketing colleague was being measured on bringing new product revenues into the business. To introduce new products the factory had to run trials and the calculation method used for the factory efficiency measure made no allowance for this. As a result, new products were the last thing that I wanted to see in the factory and so were deprioritized in the production plans, an action that upset my colleague.

There are multiple other examples we see like this in organizations we work with, where measures that have not been aligned across the organization cause not only friction but also ongoing poor performance.

Too few measures. Although too many measures drive KPI fatigue, too few can mean that poor efficiency of processes is overlooked or the costs actually involved with achieving a specific result is hidden. As an example, one client put all of its focus on its customer service performance, which most people would agree is worthy of being measured. However, this was pretty much all the client measured in the short term, and by not looking at the underlying performance of both manufacturing and logistics, the client did not realize that great customer service was being delivered only through significant expenditure on unplanned overtime and premium freight.

Measuring people not process. When you measure people, their reaction to being measured can drive irrational responses and negative emotions, including defensiveness and looking to push blame on to others. On the flip side, people may find a way to cheat or game the measure to meet the target, especially if a reward is at stake.

What to Measure and the Implementation Hierarchy

Some suggestions about the measures that should be part of the Integrated Tactical Planning process have been included in previous chapters but before we pull them together into a single list, it is important to get focused again on why we are measuring.

Over the last 50 years, the Oliver Wight organization has worked with thousands of organizations, and we have learned that as they move through the maturity journeys that we outlined in Chapter 1 the measures that they need to focus on change. We have illustrated this in Figure 6.3.

For organizations starting their improvement journey at the lowest levels of maturity, a focus on getting the basic data correct provides a vital foundation. If the data used as the basis for the plans in the execution zone are inaccurate, then the result will be invalid plans that no one believes. Despite the increasing power of integrated planning software, the adage of "garbage in, garbage out" that first surfaced in the 1960s as computers entered the mainstream society is still valid. Another symptom of poor data accuracy and plans that no one believes is the additional workload created by everyone having their own plan, because they do not trust and are second-guessing the plans generated by the planning team using their planning software.

From an improvement perspective, improving data accuracy reduces rework and thus cost. Data inaccuracy creates frustration and mistrust between functions, so addressing this improves the operating dynamics within the organization. Data accuracy is an essential foundation for excellent execution.

FIGURE 6.3 Hierarchy of Performance Measures Implementation

Source: Oliver Wight. Copyright Oliver Wight International, Inc. Used with permission.

As an organization builds confidence in its plans through ensuring the accuracy of the data that they are built on, the focus of measurement can then move to "are we doing what we said we would do?" Understanding the likelihood of the plan being executed as intended, and thus the likelihood of it not being executed as intended, triggers actions for contingencies to be put in place. If the manufacturing process meets the planned output only 90% of the time, then knowing this enables buffers to be created against this nonperformance in the form of safety stock or safety capacity as a logical contingency to maintain service to the customer or next step in the supply chain.

From an improvement perspective, "doing what we say we are going to do" reduces rework and cost because other plans do not need to be readjusted in the very short term in reaction to the nonperformance. Dealing with the consequences of poor plan execution—"not having done what we said we would do"—is probably the single largest contributor to the firefighting culture that many organizations tell us characterize their existence.

Examples of the impact of "not doing what we said we would do" abound:

- Shipments not arriving on time, resulting in alternate sources of raw material having to be procured at very short notice—in some cases necessitating changes to recipes/bills of material.

- Production schedules not being met on time, triggering overtime and/ or customer service misses.
- Products not being dispatched or delivered on time, resulting in queries from the customer as to the whereabouts of their order, subsequent checking and communication back and forth, and in some cases customer claims and dealing with customer's emotional response to "having been let down".

These chain reactions result in increased cost, and for the individuals and teams that have to do the reacting, it comes as additional work and a distraction from the work that they had planned. A salutary observation is that most organizations do not employ staff specifically to deal with and to react to plans not being executed but that many employees end up being distracted from their stated roles through having to deal with the consequences of poor execution. During a session with one of our clients, a supply chain manager, when asked to illustrate how he saw himself in the organization, drew a picture of himself wearing a fireman's helmet, blindfolded, and juggling hand grenades (see Figure 6.4)!

FIGURE 6.4 Supply Chain Manager's Self-Image

Source: Oliver Wight. Copyright Oliver Wight International, Inc. Used with permission.

Improving the reliability of execution against the plan also reduces the amount of contingency that needs to be built in to buffer the organization and/or customer against nonperformance and so reduces cost. It also builds trust, between functions, between suppliers and customers, and between business unit and the head office.

Once an organization has improved its reliability and established sustainable capability to "do what it said it would do," the measurement focus can then move to improvement and using measures to ask and answer the question, "are we getting better?"

In the context of Integrated Tactical Planning, the "are we getting better?" focus becomes "are we getting better at executing the plan?" This does not just mean "are we doing what we said we would do?" but also "how are we getting there?" One common lens through which to ask and answer this question is that of cost.

You can achieve near 100% customer service through doubling or even tripling your inventories but at what cost? Working capital, storage, obsolescence, and write-off all typically increase in such a scenario. You can achieve near 100% supply performance by reducing efficiency targets or accepting lower production rates. The result of this is typically higher unit cost.

Indicators of "are we getting better at executing our plan?" will vary from organization to organization based on business type and industry, but some examples will suffice:

- Premium freight costs (airfreight).
- Wastage/write-off costs.
- Unplanned overtime costs.
- Inventory holding costs (working capital interest, warehouse, clearance, write-off, damage).
- Customer credits.

After "are we getting better?" an organization can focus attention on "are we driving toward our strategic goals?" and "are we changing the rules?" Because these deal more with the medium- and long-term planning horizon, and not the short-term horizon of Integrated Tactical Planning, we will not expand on them further in this book, but readers interested in more information should read more about Integrated Business Planning and its role as an enabler for executives to lead an organization through change, articulate the strategy, and ensure that it is deployed.

An illustration of this suggested sequence of measurement focus is a case in which we worked with a client in the *fast-moving consumer goods (FMCG)* industry that focused on the "right measures at the right time" to rebuild trust with its major grocery customer and grow sales.

Our client was the market leader in one of the grocery retailer's "destination categories," that is, a product category that the retailer used to draw customers into its stores, in this case, primarily through aggressive price discounting. Internally our client was running a number of initiatives focused on reducing costs to increase margins and deliver on the budgeted profit number for that financial year. At this time customer service levels were running between 88% and 92% and the company was under increasing pressure from the retailer to improve because the poor service level had triggered stock shortages in the retailer's distribution centers, leading to gaps on the store shelves during key price promotions. The situation was exacerbated by a period of intense competition in the grocery retail sector that saw competing retailers using short-notice promotional activities to attempt to gain advantage over each other. The retailer's dissatisfaction and need to respond to frequent requests to "explain and improve" were diverting attention away from the cost reduction initiatives that underpinned the budgeted profit target.

Caught in the crossfire, our client was not only spending a great deal of time apologizing but also finding that the retailer was not interested in discussing their planned new products, which in the strategic plan were intended to maintain growth levels in line with global head office aspirations. The buyer at the retailer was reported as saying, "Why would we add more of your products to our range when you can't provide reliable supply of the existing ones!"

We helped the client understand and put in place sufficient contingencies in the form of additional finished goods inventory to buffer against supply nonperformance and significant short-term changes to the demand plan. Although this involved additional investment in inventory and storage, the result was that service levels were improved to consistently above 98%. The retailer's mood changed, and the door was reopened to discuss new products and partnering to jointly drive category growth. By tackling the challenge and focusing on "doing what we say we are going to do," the client reduced the internal noise associated with the previous nonperformance sufficiently to create time and head space for its employees to determine actions and commence a program of supply chain improvement that systematically reduced the costs of maintaining 98%+ service levels.

Measures for Integrated Tactical Planning

So, understanding the recommended measurement implementation hierarchy, what measures should be used to support the Integrated Tactical Planning process?

DATA MEASURES   Let's start with data as that is the foundation of the implementation hierarchy. As we have already stated, without accurate data nothing works in an ERP system. In Chapter 5 we identified static and dynamic data elements that should be measured for accuracy:

- Item master data.
- Bill of material/recipe data.
- Routing master data.
- Work center data.
- Logistics master data.
- Inventory record accuracy.
- Customer master data.
- Supplier master data.
- Price lists/product catalogs.

The Oliver Wight experience is that if data accuracy is less than 95% (except for BOMs, which should be a minimum of 98%) on an ongoing basis then two things happen:

- The level of firefighting in the organization is a significant drain on resources and morale, because employees find themselves constantly dealing with the errors that the incorrect data is driving into the ERP system. The resultant excessive _action messages_ (also known as _exception messages and alerts_) overwhelm the planners, and the incorrect recommendations trigger suboptimal actions.
- People do not trust the information in the ERP system. This results in the creation of multiple coping strategies that may include spreadsheets, additional physical checks, and in many cases, elements of the ERP system being ignored or switched off altogether.

It is a strange thing that senior executives in many organizations are prepared to allow excessive cost, stress, and the risk of poor service to their customers through not maintaining the basic data required for their planning and execution systems, which have often cost millions of dollars, to operate effectively. If these were Formula 1 racing teams, it would be like trying to race the latest multimillion-dollar car without regularly checking the oil or tire pressures and having a driver who does not trust the speedometer or rev counter.

"ARE WE DOING WHAT WE SAID WE WOULD DO?" MEASURES   Remember, these are all about monitoring execution and providing visibility of deviation from plan to allow course correction, as well as identifying nonperformance to trigger root cause analysis and permanent corrective action to be put in place.

- Key metrics for product launch readiness
  - *Product project milestones achieved on time*

      Areas of deficiency that we often see with new products are the provision of data from the project team to another function so that they have sufficient time to do their work. We touched on some of these in Chapter 4 and examples include provision of recipe information to enable the procurement team to source new raw materials and communicate the detailed launch demand plan to enable the supply organization to plan and establish supply and distribution capacity.

      Another area that is a common bottleneck in the new product introduction process and warrants measurement attention applied to the process is dealing with external suppliers; artwork and artwork approval are a common bottleneck.
  - *New product trials' success rate—on time and in full*

      This is an indicator of the likelihood of additional capacity being required to run further trials. Without this visibility there is no basis to determine whether contingencies need to be put in place to keep the execution of the product project plan on track.
  - *New product master data set up on time*

      Of all the processes that contribute to the successful launch of new products, the most common complaint we hear among clients is about delays in the data setup of new products. During a diagnostic assessment conducted for a food manufacturing company, employees from multiple functions commented that their jobs were made more difficult due to new product master data not being set up on time. Material planners could not order raw materials until recipes were set up. Production planners could not schedule production until part numbers were set up and routings and work center data established. The customer care team could not take, enter, and confirm orders until part numbers, pricing, and packing configurations were established. The delays in data setup created a time line compression that generated negative stress for individuals and in some cases drove additional costs and service issues.

      When questioned, the data governance team said that they operated to a service level agreement (SLA) of 5 days for new product setups, but in the case of products and raw materials that were new to the business, and not something already in use elsewhere in the region, that the lead time would often be more than 10 days. The performance against the SLA was not published among the internal customers who were the ones experiencing the issues and frustrations resulting from nonperformance.

- Key metrics for demand execution
  - *Demand plan variance*
    Monitoring demand—tracking consumption of the demand plan and providing alerts when action is required
  - *Execution of the sales activity plan*
    Demand does not just happen. Tracking execution of the activities that have been planned to stimulate demand can provide early warning of risks to the demand plan and trigger corrective action. Sales activities will differ from company to company and from industry to industry but could include these elements:
    - Number of sales calls made.
    - In-store merchandising activity.
    - Shelf or off location position for in-store promotion.
    - Advertising campaign execution timeliness, for example, did the retailer catalog contain our product?

    These are the activities that support the assumptions that underpin the plan, so it is important to monitor their execution.
- Key metrics for supply execution
  - *Schedule adherence*
    - Master supply plan
    - Manufacturing schedule
    - Supplier schedule
    - Warehouse schedule
    - Logistics schedule

    The focus of schedule adherence metrics is to measure the on-time and in-full completion of the discrete elements of the schedule. These could be work orders, process orders, purchase orders, transfer orders, pick and pack orders, or shipping orders (note that different ERP systems may use different terminology). Measures would typically include both the immediate period and the stability and accuracy of the 13-week plan.
  - *Aggregate supply plan performance*
    While the schedule adherence metrics measure completion of the discrete elements of the schedule or plan, the aggregate supply plan metric measures the completion of the total plan by volume.

    As an example, if a manufacturing plant completed 75 of 100 work orders that were in the plan for a specific week, on time (measured by planned completion day) and in full (measured by volume within any specified tolerance) then the schedule adherence would be 75%. If the aggregate plan for the week was 30,000 units and by

the end of the week 27,000 units had been produced the aggregate supply plan performance would be 90%.

Measuring both schedule and aggregate performance is important because the aggregate plan could be achieved by over-producing easy-to-supply products and not everything on the schedule, thus triggering potential service issues.

- *Customer delivery performance*

    This is a critical measure that underpins customer satisfaction. Although seemingly a straightforward measure of whether the product/service was delivered to the customer when we said it would be, the devil is in the details. Following are key elements to define:

    - Is the metric measuring against a promise made at the time of order confirmation, a contractual service level agreement, or a customer request?
    - Is the metric measuring shipment from the supplier or delivery to and receipt at the customer?
    - Is the metric measuring delivery at an order level or at a line item level?

    Lack of clarity about factors such as these is a common source of frustration between suppliers and customers, can consume significant resource, and in some cases masks customer dissatisfaction.

KEY CONFORMANCE MEASURES FOR THE INTEGRATED TACTICAL PLANNING PROCESS:

- *Time fence breaches*

    As we discussed in Chapter 5, changes in the emergency zone are very expensive and disruptive so measuring how often these are occurring and then determining the root cause and corrective action is a critical agenda item for Integrated Tactical Planning. If we use the firefighting analogy that we introduced at the beginning of this book, changes in the emergency zone create the largest fires.

- *Lead time exceptions*

    Lead times are a crucial part of planning systems and processes. Understanding where lead times are consistently being crashed or exceeded provides two very useful insights. First, where process lead times are being compressed can be an indicator of the risk of negative stress on employees. One example is a quality control (QC) process that has a standard lead time of 2 days and exceptions are constantly being requested to provide clearances in 4 hours. In this instance there could be increased risk of a nonconforming product being released if the QC testing is rushed or alternative testing methods are used to expedite the clearance.

Second, if lead times are consistently being compressed, it may indicate that the process has been improved by the process users and that the lead times no longer reflect reality and need to be updated. Conversely, if lead times are consistently being missed it may indicate that the process needs to be reviewed and improved or the lead times adjusted to reflect the demonstrated performance.

- *Integrated Tactical Planning governance process meeting(s) attendance*

It is important to measure the Integrated Tactical Planning process itself. A simple measure that is an effective indicator of process health is whether the key participants in the daily and weekly Integrated Tactical Planning process meetings attend. This is especially important as the new Integrated Tactical Planning process is being introduced and is not yet embedded as "the way we do things around here."

- *Integrated Tactical Planning actions completed on time in full*

Another indicator of the health of the Integrated Tactical Planning process is the measure of action items arising from the Integrated Tactical Planning meetings being completed on time in full. Initially there is a risk that the volume of actions being generated by the cross-functional team appear overwhelming as multiple opportunities for improvement are identified. This can be a big demotivating factor. Our empirical evidence is that achieving more than 80% of actions on time in full creates a motivating effect because individuals then see Integrated Tactical Planning as "getting things done."

"ARE WE GETTING BETTER?" MEASURES

- *Cost measures*

These track the significant costs associated with execution failure and/or changes to the plan involving time fence breaches and lead time exceptions, such as the following:

- Unplanned overtime cost
- Inventory obsolescence and write-off
- Airfreight or premium freight cost
- *Velocity measures*

As represented in Figure 6.5, velocity measures the ratio of value-adding time to total elapsed time for a process.

Measuring velocity for key execution processes can expose significant improvement opportunities. Not a new concept, velocity is at the core of the Lean methodology in which focus is applied to identification and elimination of waste. In our experience of working with organizations to improve

$$\text{Velocity Ratio} = \frac{\text{Time Adding Value}}{\text{Elapsed time}} \times 100\%$$

FIGURE 6.5 Process Velocity Ratio

Source: Oliver Wight. Copyright Oliver Wight International, Inc. Used with permission.

process velocity, many products and many services receive value for less than 10% of the time that they are in the value delivery systems of their companies. Techniques such as *value stream mapping* have exposed the improvement opportunities, and many organizations have made impressive strides in the application of Lean principles in order to eliminate waste and reduce the total elapsed time of both product supply and administrative processes.

There remains, however, significant opportunity in most organizations, especially in areas outside of direct manufacturing. We assisted one client, a multinational chemical coatings manufacturer, to improve the velocity of its new product introduction process. Through focused business process acceleration activities, the company was able to reduce the elapsed time of the new product introduction process, the time taken for the new product to move from idea to product launch, from 77 days to 27 days, yielding a near threefold increase in velocity from 3.9% to 11.1%.

As customers continue to look to their suppliers to become more agile, the solution is not working harder and expediting the existing processes but rather compressing process lead times through eliminating non-value-adding activities. The starting point for this improvement effort is velocity measurement.

Components of a Measure

In our experience there are a number of components that a measure should have in order to effectively drive improvement:

- **Definition**—what is being measured?
- **Purpose**—why is it being measured? What business goal or objective does this measure support?
- **Information source**—where is the source data coming from for the measure?

- **Formula**—what calculation or ratio is being used? This one is especially important when different operations are being compared to ensure that an apples-with-apples comparison is being made. Without transparency of measurement formula, inter-business rivalry can spiral into mistrust very quickly.
- **Timing and frequency of measurement**—when and how frequently should the measure be taken?
- **Reporting lead time/frequency of reporting**—what is the agreed reporting lead time, for example, measure published 24 hours after results obtained?
- **Frequency of review**—how frequently should the measure be reviewed and actions agreed?
- **Person responsible for measurement and reporting**—who is responsible for collecting the measurement, process any required calculation, create the presentation/report?
- **Measure owner (person accountable for performance)**—who is accountable for performance and taking action in the event of non-performance?
- **Targets and tolerances**—what is the target for performance and what are the tolerances for the target that have been defined for success, for example, master supply plan performance target defined as work order completed on time to the day in full + or −0.5% quantity?
- **Glide path to the target**—looking at a performance measure chart with a seemingly impossible target that is a significant stretch to current performance is a demotivator. Breaking the journey to the target down into smaller steps or a glide path enables improvement to be recognized and celebrated more frequently along the way, with the resultant positive mindset proven to generate increased creativity for improvement solutions among team members.
- **Control limits**—what are the control limits outside of which action is required?
- **Root cause analysis of nonperformance**—in the event of performance outside of control limits or the target, investigate the root cause(s) of nonperformance.
- **Corrective action plan**—time-phased corrective action plan to address the root cause(s) of nonperformance and bring performance up to, or back to, the required level.

Measures also need to evolve. One recurring issue that we see is that companies keep the same measures year after year, with a diminishing return in value. Sometimes there are performance improvements that suggest that tolerances can be reduced to drive further incremental gains. Other times the process has changed and the metric no longer provides value in the current form and needs revising. Either way, like all good policies and procedures, your measures need regular attention and review to get the most out of them.

Closing the Loop for Improvement

In Figure 6.2 we depicted the closed-loop improvement process. Measurement and reporting are the first steps toward improvement, but without root cause analysis and corrective action plans, improvement is impossible. Before we look at some of the tools that can be used for root cause analysis and corrective action, it is worth understanding how mapping a hierarchy of measures can provide a first view of the cause(s) of nonperformance.

Understanding performance measure hierarchies to identify the root cause of nonperformance

A useful exercise to understand how execution processes and measures are aligned is to map their relationship or hierarchy. Processes are often supported by subprocesses, and nonperformance in a subprocess will inevitably either affect higher-level process performance or its cost.

In Figure 6.6 we have mapped a measurement hierarchy for customer *delivery in full, on time (DIFOT)*, illustrating the subprocesses and their measures that influence the customer DIFOT outcome.

This is a simplified version to illustrate the concept. The specific subprocesses will vary from organization to organization but in every business, undertaking mapping activities to show the relationships between process

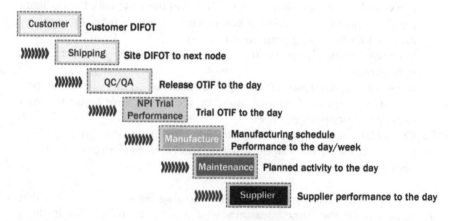

FIGURE 6.6 Customer DIFOT Measurement Hierarchy

Source: Oliver Wight. Copyright Oliver Wight International, Inc. Used with permission.

measures and their alignment will create line of sight and expose any gaps where critical-to-execution outcome subprocesses are not being measured. Constructing such performance measure hierarchies creates a solid starting point for investigating the root cause of nonperformance at any of the levels in the hierarchy.

Another benefit of this exercise is that it provides an effective communication tool to show how everyone in an organization can affect the top-level performance of the company and how departments or functions affect one another. We firmly believe that 99.9% of people come to work to do a good job but often they are let down by a lack of visibility and understanding about what is required. They use judgment and best intent based on their experience and view from their position in the organization in order to determine what is important. The understanding they obtain from the measurement hierarchy can in itself often result in improved performance as people realize that things that are not important to them are actually critical to others and the overall success of the business.

ROOT CAUSE ANALYSIS TOOLS   Over the past 30 years the business of improvement has become ever-more sophisticated with companies employing Lean and Six Sigma methodologies and expertise to drive waste and variation out of their processes. These methodologies are tremendously powerful but come at a cost in time and resources. The Black Belts and Green Belts who lead and facilitate Six Sigma activities can be an expensive resource and projects can stretch into multiple months. One negative consequence of Six Sigma methodology deployment that we have observed is the creation or reinforcement of the ideal that improvement is done for you by an "improvement expert." Although necessary and appropriate for some complex problems, this detracts from a two-job culture, in which all workers are encouraged and empowered to do their job and improve their job.

Our suggested approach for driving improvement in the Integrated Tactical Planning context is for the process users and those involved in the execution of the plans to use simple tools alongside the execution process measures to determine root causes of nonperformance, then prioritize and drive corrective action.

There are many formal tools that can be used to identify the reasons for nonperformance:

- **Charts and histograms**—display performance, targets, control limits, and performance trends.
- **Tally sheets and reason codes**—effective at capturing different types of failure or nonperformance and enables data to be stratified into meaningful categories or classifications.

- **Pareto charts**—assists in determining which problems to solve in which order by displaying the relative importance of problems in a visual format. It works on the basis of Pareto principle or the 80/20 law introduced in Chapter 2, which states that 20% of the sources cause 80% of any problem. It also enables problems to be analyzed through multiple measurement lenses, for example, frequency or cost.
- **Cause-and-effect/fishbone/Ishikawa diagrams**—assists in identifying all the possible causes related to a problem to uncover the root cause. Graphical format enables a team to explore and identify potential causes under a number of main categories to determine the most likely root cause. In a production environment the categories typically used include people, machinery/equipment, methods, materials, environment, and measurement. In a service environment the categories of policies, procedures, and equipment/space may be added or substituted.
- **Five Whys**—a technique to ask "why?" multiple times when a cause has been identified to drill down to a level that is the true reason behind the failure at a level where it can be solved. Five Whys can also be used as a follow-on from cause and effect to establish whether each cause identified is a symptom, lower-level cause, or a root cause. The technique is called the Five Whys because it often requires why? to be asked five times before the root cause is exposed.

It is important to use the tools appropriate to the size of the problem. Some of the issues you will identify at the beginning of your journey will have very obvious solutions, and you do not need to agonize in detail using these tools to solve them. Others may just need an observation. The Japanese call this a *Gemba Walk*, which literally means go to the "real place," and often by just looking, the source of issue becomes more obvious.

Whichever tools you choose to use, it is important that the people who are going to use them, the Integrated Tactical Planning team and the execution team, are educated on the basic principles. Make them easily available at point of use through printing up templates on 11 × 17 sheets or adding them to whiteboards and integrating them into the daily governance process so that they become a way of life.

One pitfall to avoid is the temptation to try and fix everything at once. Our recommendation is to use three criteria to determine what to focus on and to set priorities:

- What will provide the biggest benefit for the company? Consider this from the whole organization perspective, not just what would be best for a single function or department.

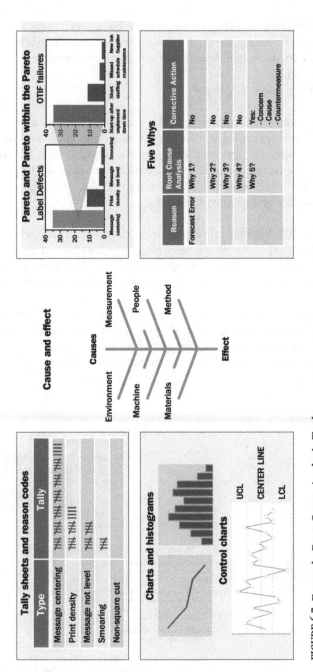

FIGURE 6.7 Example Root Cause Analysis Tools

Source: Oliver Wight. Copyright Oliver Wight International, Inc. Used with permission.

- What will provide the biggest benefit for Integrated Tactical Planning and the execution teams? At the beginning of the chapter we talked about the execution hamster wheel. What fixes will enable the team to get off the wheel?
- What will provide quick wins?

Seeing benefits created rapidly is like adding oxygen to a fire for any team involved in improvement. Proving that they can do it and that their efforts make a difference generates the positive mindset that fuels further efforts toward the next improvement. Success drives success.

Priorities for improvement should be agreed on, set, and monitored through the weekly governance meeting(s).

CORRECTIVE ACTION TOOLS   Once the root cause(s) of nonperformance have been identified, corrective action plans need to be put in place and performance of these tracked through to delivery. Visual management is an effective tool to do this, as well as for reinforcing accountability (see Figure 6.8).

The example in Figure 6.8 illustrates the components of a performance measure identified previously in the chapter and the presentation of a simple *concern—cause—countermeasure—who—when—status* matrix that turns a performance measure into a mechanism for driving performance improvement.

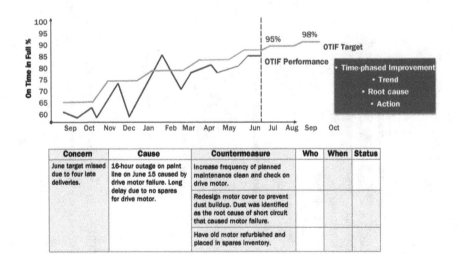

FIGURE 6.8 Performance Measure Example—Customer Service On-Time In-Full Performance

Source: Oliver Wight. Copyright Oliver Wight International, Inc. Used with permission.

Summary and Key Change Requirements

In this section we have covered the need for deliberately creating time for your employees to spend on improvement so that they can get off the execution hamster wheel. We have looked at the role that measures play in controlling and improving a process and its resulting deliverables.

We have identified measurement pitfalls to avoid and detailed a recommended hierarchy of measures implementation. Some recommended measures to be used to support the Integrated Tactical Planning process have been discussed, and we have detailed the elements of a measure framework that are required in order to truly drive performance improvement, including root cause analysis techniques and corrective action tools.

PEOPLE AND BEHAVIOR CHANGES

- People need time to undertake improvement; this needs to be planned into their work time.
- Unless execution processes are improved, people will not be able to break out of firefighting mode.
- Performance measures are a waste of time if they are not used to drive improvement—root cause analysis of nonperformance and corrective action are essential.
- Measures and targets drive behavior—measure process, not people.
- Misaligned measures will drive conflict in the organization.
- Measures, analysis, and corrective action all need to have owners.

PROCESS CHANGES

- Measures need tolerances established if they are to be used to monitor and control a process.
- Data accuracy measures provide a foundation for process performance that "are we doing what we said we would do?" and "are we getting better?" measures can then be built on.
- Establish performance measure hierarchies to identify critical to execution subprocesses.
- Root cause analysis and corrective action planning are essential components of a performance measure framework.

TECHNOLOGY CHANGES

- Measurement costs money—use technology to streamline data collection, measure presentation, and reporting.

CHAPTER 7

Running Smoothly
Structure and Cadence

A client once quipped when she was asked how she felt about the uncertainty of being recently acquired by a private equity firm, "Process is performance, and performance is protection." Although most of us shun process, especially when it is seen as overly bureaucratic and controlling, the fact is that we are in business to perform. Hence, process discipline is critical to optimal performance. We would also debate that appropriate process discipline is in fact liberating.

Think about it from a personal perspective. Without a lot of muscle memory the human body would not function properly. Imagine having to think through everything single thing you do in a day—every step you take, every word you say, every action in driving your car—every minute of the day. There must be some things done at the subconscious level to be able to get on with your day and to focus your brain power on the unique events.

Top athletes know this well. It is common for athletes, after performing at their peak, to have little memory of the specifics of how they performed. That is because their muscle memory was playing the game for them while they used their conscious brains to stay calm, focused, and continually strategizing.

This is how we see process and discipline in businesses. It is a way to do the routine things routinely and release thinking time. To achieve this level of routine, in this chapter we will cover these topics:

- The daily-weekly cadence.
- Empowerment criteria.
- Stop-and-check meetings.
- Structure.
- Leadership and roles.
- Behaviors.
- The sustainability plan (read that as making sure processes stay in good shape).

To ensure that decisions are made at the right level and in a timely manner, there are layers of process in a business as discussed in Chapter 2. These layers have a sequence of planning, communicating, executing the plans, measuring, learning, applying the learning, and (re)planning in a never-ending cycle (see Figure 7.1).

From the monthly Integrated Business Planning process to the weekly Integrated Tactical Planning process—this means aligning on what marketing is going to promote, what sales is going to sell, what customer service is going to promise, what supply chain planning is going to plan, what production is going to make, and what purchasing is going to buy.

Because this is a cycle of replanning, each layer of process needs to routinely stop and review to make sure everyone is realigned with the latest situation and latest plans. As a marketing director once said about his organization, "It's like continental drift; if we don't routinely stop and bring everyone back together, they'll just slowly and imperceivably drift apart to such an extent that by the time we realize it's happened, the distance will have become so great that it becomes a massive chore to pull it all back into alignment."

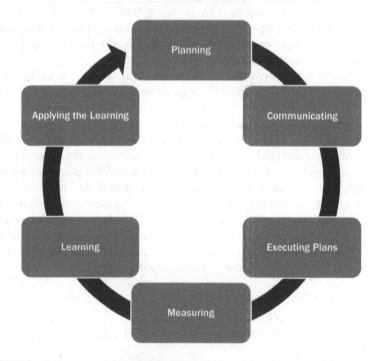

FIGURE 7.1 Planning and Replanning Cycle

Source: Oliver Wight. Copyright Oliver Wight International, Inc. Used with permission.

These stop and reviews are routine meetings that need to have a clear purpose, which is to understand what has changed since last time and realign everyone on the new plans. It needs to be built into the DNA of the organization to ensure there is always transparency and alignment to one set of plans and numbers. As we described previously, strategy sets the organization's strategic road maps, the 3-year business plan sets the actions in place to deliver the road maps, and the Integrated Business Planning process operationalizes the two to three business plans. The Integrated Tactical Planning process then controls execution of the first 3 months of the Integrated Business Planning process, and the daily execution meetings keep track on delivering the weekly plans. This is the essence of a closed-loop planning system.

It sounds all very top-down and one way, doesn't it? Well, it's not. The next step is keeping the loop closed, by bottom-up processes, to loop back up, as Figure 7.2 depicts.

The Daily-Weekly Cadence

The daily cadence starts with the monitoring of daily sales to ensure the organization is on track to deliver the weekly demand plan. This is one of the tasks of the demand execution manager and requires liaising with sales and customer service on a routine basis to understand the trends, determine how to respond to deviations, and work with the master supply planner/ scheduler to agree on suitable responses.

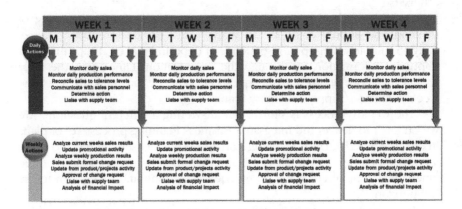

FIGURE 7.2 The Daily-Weekly Cadence

Source: Oliver Wight. Copyright Oliver Wight International, Inc. Used with permission.

At the same time, the master supply planner/scheduler will be monitoring daily production (in a manufacturing organization) or supplier delivery performance (in a supply chain business) to track progress to the weekly supply plans. The planner will routinely be liaising with production, material planners, distribution planners, and purchasing to agree on responses to deviations and ultimately with the demand execution manager to give early warnings of potential stock shortages or excesses.

A demand execution manager in a pharmaceutical company told us a funny story about the company's medical director. The medical director stopped to have a chat one day and asked about what he was doing. The demand execution manager said that he was checking daily sales against the forecast. The medical director, who had previously made it quite clear to everyone that he was "indifferent" to sales and marketing, said, "I can't get too excited about what we're selling; I've got too many other important things to do." The demand execution manager spun around and said in response, "If we're not selling to plan, then you're not going to get your bonus!" The demand execution manager later said, "That was the worst thing I've ever done—now the medical director comes to me every single day and quizzes me on sales, and if we're not tracking too well, he'll be back at lunch, and then as he's leaving for the day . . . maybe he should stick to his more important things!"

The point being that someone needs to be monitoring what is being executed to keep the senior team out of the detail, as we discussed previously in the book. Hence the escalation criteria, which we will talk about later in this chapter, needs to be set up so that senior management can be confident that everything is on track, unless they formally hear otherwise.

Depending on the size of the organization, the daily monitoring of demand and supply could be an activity and progress report, a single, daily 15-minute catch-up or a sequence of departmental catch-ups that filter important information up through the organization. Either way, the daily routine is about answering the question, "Are we on track to meet the weekly demand/supply/inventory plans?"

The weekly process is similar, but answering a different question: "Are we on track to deliver the Integrated Business Planning process set of plans in our Integrated Tactical Planning horizon?" The data set will need to cover a horizon of at least 13 weeks, and, although there is a special focus on the emergency zone, there needs to be equal weighting and time given to the full horizon.

Changes to the product, demand, supply, and inventory plans out to the planning time fence form the core elements of the Integrated Tactical

Planning meeting(s). Other topics are plan change approvals, contingency plans, and any potential impact on the financial plans. The key actions arising from the weekly Integrated Tactical Planning meetings are plans to close the gaps to plans, issues that cannot be resolved, and the need for escalation for approval or a decision.

Figure 7.3 is an example of a daily governance process from a global FMCG (fast-moving consumer goods) client, who has many sites/nodes and a large *distribution network*. Their customer base is volatile due to the heavily promotions-driven supermarket customers. They therefore need to keep close to stock levels and the daily order patterns. As you can see it is coordinated into 15-minute, 30-minute at most, huddles, with a specific purpose of ensuring everything is on plan. This may sound like a lot of coordination, but remember, this is an exception-based process, which means it has to be assumed that we had a good plan yesterday, so let's just address what has changed and whether we need to do anything about correcting the plan.

The daily process is a drumbeat—it should just happen without thinking. It does, however, need to be aligned with delivering to the weekly plans so that issues can seamlessly feed the weekly process without panic or fanfare. This weekly process then has its own cadence as shown in Figure 7.4.

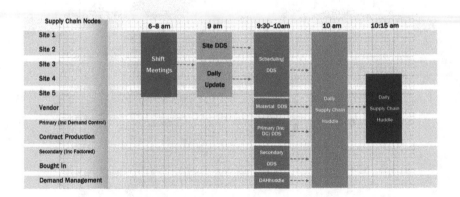

FIGURE 7.3 Daily Governance

Source: Oliver Wight. Copyright Oliver Wight International, Inc. Used with permission.

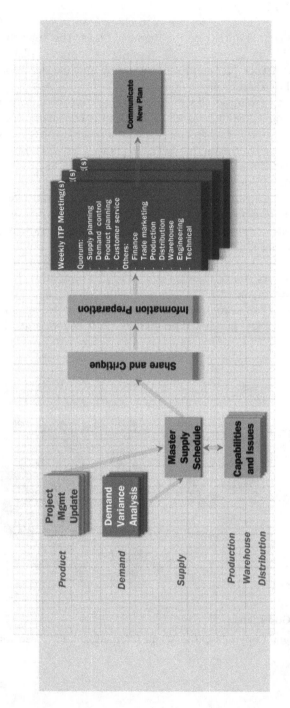

FIGURE 7.4 Example of the Weekly Planning Process and the Integrated Tactical Planning Meeting

Source: Oliver Wight. Copyright Oliver Wight International, Inc. Used with permission.

The typical flow in a relatively simple, single-site organization might be something like this:

Friday:
- AM: update and share the product portfolio plan.
- PM: run the demand variance report and share the impact on the next 13 weeks.

Monday:
- AM: regenerate the master schedule with any demand changes and test the impact with a weekly rough-cut capacity plan out for the next 13 weeks.
- PM: sign off all change approvals.

Tuesday:
- AM: regenerate lower-level plans, that is, distribution, material, shop-floor, and purchasing.
- PM: share the new supply plans with production, distribution, and purchasing.

Wednesday:
- AM: receive feedback.
- PM: create and share the weekly meeting information pack.

Thursday:
- AM: run the Integrated Tactical Planning meeting.
- PM: publish new plans and the Integrated Tactical Planning meeting summary one-pager.

Friday: AM: start again.

Figure 7.5 gives an example of a bigger and more complex company with multiple sites and products. This is the same company as in Figure 7.3, and, as you can see, even in complex organizations, the overlap between daily and weekly can be effectively sequenced, as long as the objectives and outputs are clear.

In this example, the supply chain nodes have their weekly partnership meetings through the week. The output from this is combined with the weekly actual sales data to feed into the commercial review the following Monday. This then closes the loop on the layers of plans with the intent to communicate bad (or good) news early. Figure 7.6 shows the layers of process from the monthly Integrated Busines Planning process, down to daily execution, and the way they are interconnected via looping back at the end of each period—daily, weekly, monthly—to check on progress to the higher-level plan.

As mentioned previously in the book, no organization that we have ever worked with has more resources than they need to get things done,

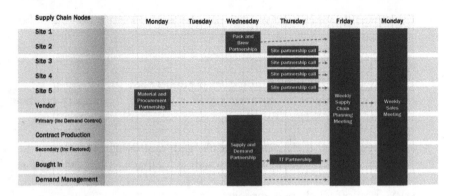

FIGURE 7.5 Example Weekly Governance Complex Organization

Source: Oliver Wight. Copyright Oliver Wight International, Inc. Used with permission.

and hence there are always going to be trade-off decisions to make. Leaders need to be accountable for delivery of their respective plans and **being over** the detail, but importantly, not **being in** the detail. The quorum or process facilitators should be responsible for early identification of changes to plans, managing the responses to correct their plans within their respective horizon, and escalation through the organization if that is not possible.

There are three important characteristics of a closed-loop planning system: roles, empowerment, and early-warning mechanisms. The roles element we described previously in the book as the quorum is responsible for maintaining the integrity of their respective execution processes and plans. Empowerment is driven through decision rights and an agreed-on and formal escalation policy, which defines what can be done by the quorum itself, as well as being clear on the triggers for when an escalation is required. The third characteristic of early warning mechanisms is a behavior that needs to be ingrained in everyone participating in the process. There needs to be a move away from knee-jerk reaction and toward anticipation. In many companies that react to bad news by shooting the messenger, people are more inclined to keep quiet. Encouraging anticipation and early communication of potential changes gives the organization time to respond appropriately and consider all the implications. Some of us who were in manufacturing used to have a process called the *anticipated delay report,* but regardless of what it is called today or what technology is available to facilitate this, there needs to be a mechanism and cultural attitude to drive buying time.

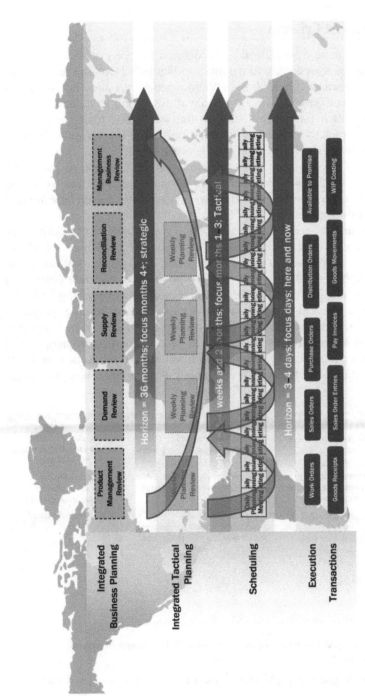

FIGURE 7.6 Monthly-Weekly-Daily Processes Need Formal Architecture to Run in Parallel and Remain Aligned

Source: Oliver Wight. Copyright Oliver Wight International, Inc. Used with permission.

Empowerment Criteria

The empowerment criteria need to be defined in terms of what decisions can be made by specific job functions, and Figure 7.7 outlines an example of what the criteria might look like. Without setting up these criteria, many companies either have the wrong people at the wrong level, making decisions outside their pay grades, such as the warehouse manager deciding who to send stock to in times of limited supply, or at the opposite extreme, every decision about changes to plans gets escalated.

Figure 7.7 shows three levels of escalation from minor, to moderate, to major, and we are sure you can think of many examples that would fall naturally into each classification. The two primary criteria used here are cost and metric performance.

With regards to cost, this is something the company has to define. For example, a company we worked with who made concrete pipes set its cost threshold at $50,000, which was a shock when we first heard it, but as the company explained, "It costs that much to put a set of concrete pipes on a truck, so anything less than that and we'd be escalating everything." Another company that was a third-party manufacturer of biscuits became quite anxious about anything over $1,000. These decisions should also be supported by a process to capture, track, and report on the number of changes and cost over time because it is important to have information to be able to do root cause analysis on the source of changes. For example, was the change

	Type of Change	Tolerances	Authorisation
Inside the Planning Time Fence	Minor changes in demand or supply	Less than $?? Within key measure tolerances	Supply scheduler Demand execution manager Line supervisor
	Moderate change that may cost money, cut into safety, or affect an A customer	Within +/−$?? cost Key measures may be affected	Sales director Finance director Supply chain director
	Major change that will cost significant money or have a big impact on customer service	Greater than $?? Considerable impact on customer service and financial projections	CEO and lead team

• Requires change form to document reasons and plan
• Analysis on the number and type of changes
• Documented and communicated management plan

FIGURE 7.7 Example Decision Rights Designed to Empower People to Make Decisions

Source: Oliver Wight. Copyright Oliver Wight International, Inc. Used with permission.

driven by demand, internal supply, or external supply? The paradigm is usually that most change is demand driven, but often we find a broader spread of causes.

The key metrics for the Integrated Tactical Planning process were defined in Chapter 6 and cover our ability to plan and execute to those plans effectively. Each of these metrics will be defined by a tolerance or control limits, and as long as the metric is still going to be delivered within these parameters, then the planners can go ahead and make the change. However, when it becomes obvious that these tolerances are going to be breached, it is the natural trigger to formally review and respond. For example, a manufacturing metric—schedule adherence—is often defined as "completing a run of finished products, on time, in full, within +/−5% on volume." In this case it is clear that the manufacturing run can go a little over or a little short and there will be no material impact to any other area of the business.

The other characteristic is that the escalation process needs to have clear guidelines on decision turnaround time. For example, if you only have a short window from order receipt to dispatch, then you need a very quick process without the bureaucracy. In one company, they defined the turnaround time for a "moderate" issue (see Figure 7.7) as 4 hours, or same day, whichever was shortest. Major issues, however, might need a little longer to work around the problem.

These characteristics take a little time to hone. In the start-up period there will be issues that arise that are shades of gray. In most companies, that usual response to a gray area is to either ignore it and hope it goes away or to act and hope you don't have to apologize later. However as one integration lead commented on this issue, "I used to be a zealot with this stuff initially, in that any gray issue that would come up, I'd note it down and in our weekly program meetings, discuss how we handled it, what we would have done differently, and agree how the escalation criteria should be changed. Although it took about 3 months to get it down to virtually no gray issues coming in anymore, it was worth the time, because everyone just knows it now and there is no hesitation. We do, however, continue to review all our policies every year, so it gets another once over then, too."

Stop-and-Check Meetings

We spoke previously about the process and the matrix of reviews, but it is also important to understand the meeting characteristics. Although the data sourcing, information collation, and decision-making may require some system sophistication, the thinking does not have to be so, and the emphasis should be on keeping it short and sweet and as simple as possible.

Although it is good to keep it simple, there needs to be discipline in following the agenda, maintaining accurate and timely data, and ensuring decisions are made at the lowest possible level in the business. Figure 7.8 show examples of the daily and weekly agendas. There is also room to highlight the monthly agenda, which is a bit too broad to go into here, but once those three layers are aligned in objectives, decision-making, and respective horizon, the loop is then fully closed from strategy to execution and back.

The other behavior shift to understand is that these gatherings are just a stop and check **within a process**. As one client mentioned, he used to call these meetings the "Oh no! meetings" (or similar), because 2 hours before the meeting, he would get the minutes from the last meeting and go, "Oh no! I haven't done what I said I was going to do!"—which indicates the process has not been well defined or deployed. The thinking is often, just put another meeting in and it will fix our planning and execution problems. Unfortunately, it is never that simple. It is the process that is more important and needs mapping out.

A useful technique to map the process and meetings is what is known as a SIPOC chart, which standards for, a *supplier* of *input* to a *process* (or meeting in this case) that has an *output* that goes to a *customer* of that output, and that customer agrees that it is in a useful format.

Figure 7.9 shows a generic template for designing the process. This one includes the SIPOC process elements, which captures roles and

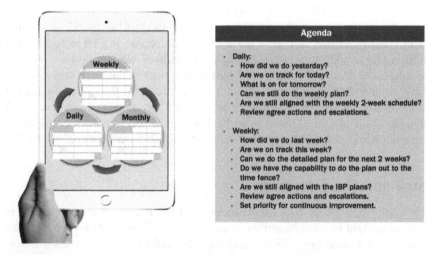

FIGURE 7.8 Weekly-Daily Integration via Aligned Meeting Agendas

Source: Oliver Wight. Copyright Oliver Wight International, Inc. Used with permission.

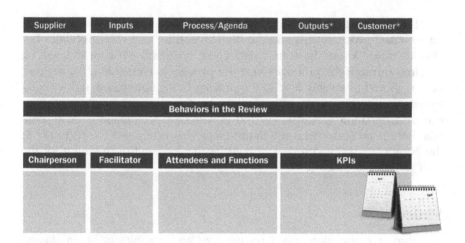

FIGURE 7.9 SIPOC Chart of Mapping Processes and Meeting

Source: Oliver Wight. Copyright Oliver Wight International, Inc. Used with permission.

responsibilities by default through the suppliers, customers, and the attendee's boxes, and has space for expected behaviors and key metrics.

The other way to use the SIPOC format is dropping down a layer from the swim lanes used in Figures 7.3, 7.4, and 7.5, and converting them into a sideways SIPOC for mapping out what gets done day to day (see Figure 7.10). This is a client example layout, and although the headings are a little different, the intent is the same.

Detailed Process SIPOC
Integrated Tactical Planning Process

	Step 1	Step 2	Step 3	Step 4	Step 5	Step 6	Step 7	Step 8
Supplier								
Input								
Process Activities (Agenda)					ITP Weekly Meeting			
System/ files/data locations								
Measures								
Outputs								
Timing	Monday AM	Monday PM	Tuesday AM	Wednesday PM	Thursday AM	Thursday PM	Friday AM	Friday PM

FIGURE 7.10 Sideways SIPOC

Source: Oliver Wight. Copyright Oliver Wight International, Inc. Used with permission.

The advantage of the sideways SIPOC is that it not only captures the time-phased process steps and the high-level roles and responsibilities but also identifies where the source data come from and what metrics will be required through the process. Once the process is embedded, this style of design should ultimately lead to the process being automated and working to remove the reliance on individuals to be constantly chasing up information and updating spreadsheets and PowerPoint presentations. Also, note that there is no customer listed in this table; that is because the customer of the outputs, in a flow process, should be the recipient of the input for the next step in the process.

Structure

Structure is highly dependent on the size and complexity of an organization. The default structure is straightforward in that there will be one monthly Integrated Business Planning process and one weekly Integrated Tactical Planning process, and in many smaller organizations, that may be the most effective approach.

However, life is usually not that simple. In bigger organizations there needs to be a bit more thinking put into the structure. The complexity of the product/distribution/customer/supplier base, and the geographical spread of business entities, usually mean several Integrated Tactical Planning processes are needed to work in parallel.

In one global business we worked with, it was such a diverse business that almost every conceivable structural difference was represented, from channel to commodity to category to country.

So how do you go about assessing how to structure the interfacing between the monthly Integrated Business Planning process and the potentially several weekly Integrated Tactical Planning processes? Let's start with a reminder that the Integrated Business Planning process is an *aggregate business planning* and management framework, which means it is deliberately designed not to operate at a detailed level. Integrated Tactical Planning is meant to operate at a more detailed level, and therefore one process usually cannot manage the depth of information required.

Following are some guidelines for assisting in making decisions on how to structure the process. The first step is to do the numbers. The key ones are how many SKUs, customers, suppliers, supply points, channels, and categories. The larger the number, the more likely it is to need more than one Integrated Tactical Planning process. The interesting point is that it doesn't have to be aligned to size of revenue or profit. For example, one global company only had 75 SKUs and 15 distributors, so it was easily managed in one process.

The second step is to understand and align with the go-to-market approach, and indeed, one of our clients was aligned from the marketing categories through to their several manufacturing facilities, which made it easy to set up their Integrated Tactical Planning processes aligned by category, with one extra one for the export channel. Alignment like this, however, is not often found. Following on from category, the next most often seen structure is by channel, which might be, for example, retail and B2B, as in a petroleum and lubrication business.

The third approach is geographically based, as seen in a large pharmaceutical company we worked with where their Integrated Tactical Planning processes were aligned by country.

Whatever the final structure turns out to be, if more than one process is required, it is often referred to as a matrix because each process needs to be defined, not only in terms of what that process is covering but also how it then relates to other Integrated Tactical Planning processes and Integrated Business Planning processes. Also, as the example matrix in Figure 7.11 depicts, it is often the case that the structure will be a hybrid of category, channel, distribution center, and manufacturing sites.

In most cases, the structural question can be addressed at the design and deployment stage. It is highly recommended that deployment follow Oliver Wight's Proven Path (this has been dealt with in many previous

Example Integrated Tactical Planning Matrix

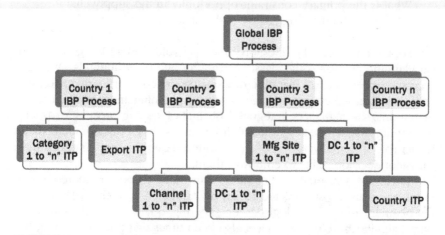

FIGURE 7.11 Example Integrated Tactical Planning Matrix

Source: Oliver Wight. Copyright Oliver Wight International, Inc. Used with permission.

publications, so we will not go further into detail here), which recommends a pilot, bullet proofing, and rollout approach. This means that a segment of the business is chosen to pilot the design. In most cases, this pilot will, in its early stages of design and testing, shed more light on refining the initial recommendations as based on the guidelines previously mentioned.

The good news is that weekly cadence creates a wave of energy, resulting in an ability to learn and apply that learning rapidly and drive a faster realization of benefits. It is important to recognize, however, that there needs to be a sustainability plan and a solid overarching Integrated Business Planning process in place to continue the flow of benefits for the longer term.

Leadership and Roles

In Chapter 2 we discussed the quorum that forms the nucleus of the Integrated Tactical Planning process, but there are others to consider, such as who will lead the Integrated Tactical Planning process.

Apart from the experience and leadership characteristics that any leader role would require, the rationale behind choosing the right Integrated Tactical Planning process leader needs to be assessed on what type of decisions the company wants the team to make. The following criteria are a good starting point:

- What is the company's go-to-market strategy and *value proposition*?
- What is the primary constraint/opportunity in the supply chain?
- Where are the most significant costs incurred?

So, the answer to the question of who should lead an Integrated Tactical Planning process is the classic consulting one of "it depends." We have seen Integrated Tactical Planning process leaders come from demand managers/demand execution managers, supply planning managers, customer operations, site managers, Integrated Business Planning process leads, and distribution managers. For sustainability, however, the critical issue is that a leader role is formally assigned, along with the quorum, and that they have sufficient decision rights to empower them.

There are also other stakeholders who need to be considered. Often input plans are mostly related to supply, and hence roles such as material planners, purchasing, logistics, engineering, quality, and operations can play a significant role. There have also been times that trade marketing has played a significant role in highly promotionally sensitive environments, or regulatory in the pharmaceutical industry, or even legal in environments that have a significant contract base for their sales. Finance is also beginning to play a bigger role in that people in that department can assist with understanding the cost trade-offs with managing changes to plans, identifying the profit implications of mix variance, and evaluating the financial impacts of simulating various scenarios.

The important point is that senior managers should not be routinely engaged in the process or meeting. They should be engaged in signing off the process design, policies, and consulted on escalations, but never getting into the day-to-day running of the Integrated Tactical Planning process. The people involved should be the people with their fingers on the pulse, who know the detail, and who are responsible for executing the plans.

What needs to be kept in mind is that the leadership team have already signed off the core and associated plans through the Integrated Business Planning process. Therefore, the assumption is that as long as the Integrated Tactical Planning team can rebalance plans back to the first 3 months of that plan, then the company is still on track.

Behaviors

In simple terms, culture could be described as collective behaviors that have served the organization well to date and have become so embedded that they become almost impossible to describe once you've been in the organization for a period of time. As anyone who has led or been engaged in a transformation journey will attest, changing the culture and embedding new behaviors in an organization is no easy feat.

Doing something new will always require some level of behavior change, and it will almost always be a change in culture that is needed. Although change can be hard, starting does not have to be. Change is either driven by the vision of what life could be like or a deep dissatisfaction with how things are now. So, a good starting point is to simply write down what you want to be and then write down what you are now. A past client made the comment, "That seems all too hard and I'm not sure there is any benefit in it." It was not obvious to him that he had lost the ability to see the embedded behaviors, so we reframed the task by asking him to write down what irked him. That stimulated a roll of thoughts, such as people being late for meetings, not doing what they said they were going to do, taking a discretionary attitude as to whether or not they were going to get involved in company-sponsored initiatives, and even not really caring about what goes into role descriptions. He was left with it and came back a week later and said, "It's like wearing special spectacles that uncover the real culture, and I've now got a page full of things I'd like to change, and I now know what I want it to look like in the future."

So, although we can't do the analysis of what your culture is like in this book, we can paint a picture of what we'd like to see in a robust Integrated Tactical Planning process:

- The guiding plans are the first 3 months of the plans signed off through the most recent Integrated Business Planning cycle.
- Empowerment is with the quorum to replan as things change and use the escalation only when needed.
- Make the planning system sweat to provide accurate and timely data.
- The plans are weekly rolling plans out to at least a 13-week horizon.
- Exception management is practiced, which means focusing only on what has changed since last week.
- Do not reinvent new processes and forums to manage crises—focus on elevating the integrity and visibility of the process and quorum to manage crises.
- Drive the learning back into the process to continually elevate performance.
- To keep the executive out of the detail, practice "silence is approval."
- Set up early-warning mechanisms to flag potential delays and opportunities.
- Measure process and data performance to drive certainty of planning through to execution.
- Leverage cross-functional forums for problem-solving.
- Formalize the process and use the policies and procedures for induction education to ensure sustainability.
- Be proactive in sharing good or bad news early to enable a timely response.

The last word on structure and cadence is that we want to embed this new way of working into the very fabric of the organization, but we also do not want to lose sight of the cultural implications of embedding it so deep that people can not see it anymore. The sustainability plan will show how we can embed, sustain, and deploy improvements, all at the same time.

The Sustainability Plan

Process sustainability—why does it matter? After all, once a company has deployed the process, achieves its goals, and has reaped the benefits, there is nothing more to do, right? Wrong. Process sustainability is a crucial element in the success story and presents three significant benefits:

- Ongoing benefit realization.
- Prevention of regression and atrophy over time.
- Creating a solid platform for building further improvements.

As Oliver Wight has shown over the last five decades, one of the critical elements that sets companies apart from the also rans is discipline. The following five keys of sustainability are a self-perpetuating cycle to not only maintain the results but also continually build improvement through the application of a disciplined approach.

We often come across the misperception that the formality and discipline required for sustainability can stifle creativity and flexibility. Our experience is the opposite—it liberates creativity because there are boundaries to work within and a structure through which to get things done. The primary impact of process sustainability mechanics is to ensure that the routine things are done routinely, which in turn frees people to be innovative and creative in problem-solving and opportunity realization. However, the people-dependent processes that dominate many business cultures often result in employees—including senior managers—being dragged down by the detail and losing sight of the bigger picture.

Imagine that a new employee who joins the organization is not familiar with the process, has not received training, and doesn't understand the objectives. Unintentionally and without any malice, that person is likely to either give it lip service or invent his or her own way of doings things and end up corrupting the process and outcomes along the way. Sustainability, therefore, is a critical element.

Here are the five keys to sustainability (see Figure 7.12):

- Education and training.
- Communication and feedback.
- Formality and discipline.
- Role descriptions aligned with process.
- Appraisal and the reward and recognition approach aligned with role descriptions.

Let's drop into a bit more detail of each.

Education and Training

The first point of contact for someone new to the business should be the induction program, but unfortunately many companies' induction programs miss out on the business management framework. A client recently mentioned, "My process induction was a couple of minutes with my boss, and then straight into my first meeting to 'learn by doing.'" Most companies have induction education, but rarely does it cover company business planning frameworks such as Integrated Tactical Planning. Although broader than just

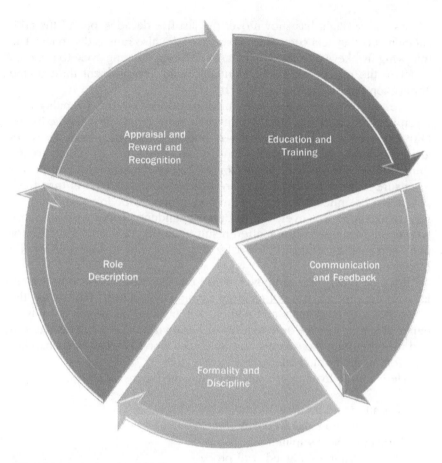

FIGURE 7.12 Five Keys to Sustainability

Source: **Oliver Wight. Copyright Oliver Wight International, Inc. Used with permission.**

Integrated Tactical Planning, a company induction program should cover at least the following:

- Integrated Business Planning process, including the decision authorization policy.
- Integrated Tactical Planning process, including time fence management and escalation criteria.
- Strategy development and deployment processes.
- Continuous improvement methodology and housekeeping process.
- Key metrics used to monitor business performance.

If the Integrated Tactical Planning process is indeed applying the learning and evolving over time, then an annual refresher should be part of the education plan. Annual refresher education sessions are golden opportunities to reenergize people by demonstrating how much has changed and improved and how much more can be achieved. It is also an opportunity to solicit feedback on refinements and improvements, and it can be timed to coincide with annual document reviews and updates to policies and procedures. Also, knowledge does fade over time, so a top-up session is always beneficial to keep things fresh and top of mind.

Although often used synonymously there is a difference between "education" and "training." Education is about the why, and training is about the how. It has been reported that typically less than 20% of businesses' ERP system functionality is being used. Because ERP systems can often be one of the single most expensive purchases for a company, running into tens of millions of dollars, it also makes it one of the single biggest wastes. It boils down to a lack of adequate training. A common mistake is for organizations to either provide superficial training—screenshots in a PowerPoint presentation—or to provide access to the tools with no guidelines at all. It is essential that not only are the tools installed to support process but also that they are used, and used optimally. Without ongoing training in the application of what is available and how it should be applied, the pernicious spreadsheet culture will infiltrate and undo a lot of the benefits that specific-purpose software provide.

Communication and Feedback

Most people think of communication as one way, but from an Oliver Wight perspective, it is two way. A good way to start is with routine process feedback, which is a form of closing the loop in establishing a culture of two-way communication. Feedback mechanisms should be in place for these times:

- The weekly Integrated Tactical Planning meeting, which is usually a one-page summary shared with key stakeholders.
- Change requests and authorizations.
- Escalations of decisions.
- Publication of key metrics, root cause analysis, and corrective action.

The routine communication ensures that people know what is going on within the process and have an opportunity to give feedback. To drive development and improvement you need to assess the performance and actively look for opportunities to improve. Mechanisms for this include applying a meeting critique and introducing periodic process reviews, but as ever, it is not the task of just doing these but the application of the learning that is the route to success.

Formality and Discipline

For sustainability to happen, policies and procedures are a fundamental and essential discipline. The value of formality is that it captures knowledge, which is used for education, and can guide all employees who subsequently join the company. When continuous improvement methodologies were first introduced decades ago, there was a simple Three Cs concept of formally managing change: challenge, change, control (see Figure 7.13).

Control is equivalent to policy and procedure—there has been a challenge to the way people work, a change for the better has been made, and now it needs to be kept in control. An analogy to illustrate this is pushing a ball upstairs, because performance improvements tend to be in steps rather than a straight line. First, the ball needs to be pushed up one step at a time, and once the right level of height has been achieved, which equates to the performance required, a chock is put in behind the ball to make sure it doesn't roll back down. The chock is policy and procedure—it stops the organization from regressing back to the bottom of the stairs.

The definition of policy and procedure vary widely from company to company, and source to source, but there are some basic guidelines. Policies are the rules by which the business is run and can only be signed off

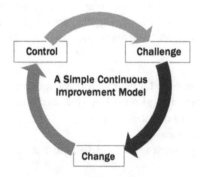

FIGURE 7.13 A Simple Change Management Approach

Source: Oliver Wight. Copyright Oliver Wight International, Inc. Used with permission.

by the CEO and the leadership team. They are the driving force behind improvement, providing the vision for the future and establishing the ambition against which all forthcoming success will be measured. They should also be brief—somewhere between three and five pages—and at least cover roles, responsibilities and accountabilities, and statements of intent.

Although the usual title is policy and procedure, it really should be policy, flow map, and procedure. The process flow map is designed to quickly and visually communicate how the process flows from beginning to end. In fact, some of the best procedures we have seen are just layered process flow maps, which combine both the detailed step-by-step instructions with a simple graphical presentation.

Procedures outline the detailed steps and are owned and managed by the process owner and users of the process—not the CEO or lead team. Many years ago, this was often a wordy document, but with modern graphical tools, today's procedures can, and should be, highly graphical.

Last, there must be an effective document-control process in place to ensure policies and procedures are kept current, relevant, and are of use to people.

Role Descriptions Aligned with Process

According to one supply chain director, "I don't see the need for role descriptions. They restrict flexibility and I can't get the most out of my people if we 'box' them in." However, firsthand experience supports the opposite. The more that expectations are aligned, the better the outcomes and the more creativity is generated because people know the boundaries in which they exist and where they can have autonomy. Achieving alignment is an active and ongoing process, and role descriptions are a good way of aligning expectations.

However, the key alignment that needs to be made in a process-sustainability context is to join the dots from the roles defined in policy to what is identified in the role description. This assists in performance appraisals, because it is fairer (and easier) to appraise against specific roles, responsibilities, and accountabilities.

Let us digress a little and define the differences among the terms *role*, *responsibility*, and *accountability*. They are often used as being the same, but they are quite different.

Role is the what a person (or what a group of people) does. For example, the role of demand execution manager is to ensure there is a process for picking up early variances to forecast and managing the implications.

Responsibility is how the person performs his or her role. To continue the example for the demand execution manager, the responsibilities might include these:

- Run daily and weekly demand variance reports.
- Report forecasting insights to demand review.
- Liaise with customer service re abnormal demand identification and management.
- Participate in the weekly Integrated Tactical Planning process.

Accountability is the measurement. For the demand execution manager, accountabilities might be defined as:

- Number of customer-driven order changes.
- Number of sales-driven forecast changes.

Although role descriptions should be tied to policies and procedures, they can often be isolated and disconnected documents. As one senior manager commented, "We only use role descriptions as a tool for placing advertisements for recruitment and nothing more." As a starting point, a useful technique for mapping the integration of roles is to use a RACI chart. It succinctly captures the cross-functionality of the process and the expectations and deliverables by role via a table identifying who is responsibility, who is accountability, who should be consulted, and who should be informed. Figure 7.14 is an example of the abnormal demand management process at order intake.

RACI Matrix: Abnormal Demand Management at Order Intake								
Deliverable (or Activity) — Role	Customer Service Lead	Customer Service Team	Global Demand Controller	Global Supply Planner	Supply Site Planners	Area Sales Director	Commercial Director	Area Sales Teams
Identification of abnormal demand.	A	R	I					
Consultation with supply chain or commercial teams as appropriate.	A	R			I	I	I	I
Execution of agreed actions through order intake process.	A	R			I	I	I	I
Escalate unresolved issues to Global Demand Controller.	A/R	C/I	I	I	I	C/I	I	C/I
Resolution of escalated unresolved issues.	C/I	C/I	R	C/I	I	I	A	I

FIGURE 7.14 Example RACI for Abnormal Demand Management at Order Intake

Source: Oliver Wight. Copyright Oliver Wight International, Inc. Used with permission.

Appraisals and the Recognition and Reward Approach Aligned with Role Descriptions

It is hardly surprising that people are heavily influenced by the way they are recognized and rewarded. A phrase often used in Oliver Wight coaching is, "If you measure people irrationally, they will behave irrationally." In other words, if given the choice, people will always choose the path that will earn them the most recognition and reward.

One Oliver Wight associate recalls, "As a young manager, I was asked to play a major role in the Integrated Tactical Planning process, as well as leading improvements in system support. When things got tough, however, and a choice had to be made between my daytime job and the process role, I chose my day job because that's what I was going to be assessed on."

When applied in an Integrated Tactical Planning process context, this means that process and behavioral expectations have been defined, they are aligned with the policies and procedures, and then they are used for people's performance appraisals. If the role description is not aligned or actively used, then there is a risk that people will not be committed to their roles in the process, because they receive neither recognition nor reward.

Summary and Key Change Requirements

In this chapter we have covered the key elements from process definition to sustainability. We have looked at what excellence in the daily and weekly meeting looks like, how the process flows week to week, and identified the key behavioral expectations.

Emphasis has been on ensuring formality and discipline of process and freeing people from people-dependent processes and using that time for problem-solving and being innovative in improving performance.

Supporting this, the decision-making criteria needs to be well defined for people to be empowered to make decisions at their level without extra approvals, but also to understand and use the trigger points to know when, how, and to whom to engage in an escalation.

Finally, we need to tie it all together with a sustainability framework to embed this knowledge in the way of workings for the business and also by routinely capturing feedback, injecting refresher programs, ensuring ongoing process communication, and not allowing the organization to be blindsided by believing the process is as good as it is ever going to be.

PEOPLE AND BEHAVIOR CHANGES
- It is a cross-functional middle management process.
- Senior managers and the executive team must trust that if they hear nothing, everything is on plan.

- Discipline in process adherence liberates time for problem-solving and innovation.
- The guiding plans are the first 3 months of the Integrated Business Planning plans.
- Drive the empowerment to the quorum to replan as things change and know when to escalate.
- Exception management is practiced, which means to focus only on what has changed since last week.
- Drive the learning back into the process to continually elevate performance.
- Formalize the process and use for induction education to ensure sustainability.

PROCESS CHANGES
- The plans are weekly rolling plans out to at least a 13-week horizon.
- Set up early-warning mechanisms to anticipate delays and plan for opportunities.
- Measure process and data accuracy performance to drive certainty of planning through to execution.
- Process structure is dependent on organization structure and go-to-market strategy.

TECHNOLOGY CHANGES
- Set up to assist with workflow alignment.
- Make the planning system sweat to provide accurate and timely data.

CHAPTER 8

Time to Releasing Value

A *Case Study in Speed to Results*

There are a number of case studies we can draw on, but we have decided that one in particular, for the sake of company confidentiality, Company X, is the one that had it all. At the time of engaging with Company X, the company had already dubbed itself the "the perfect storm," so that gives you an indication of what it was going through in the early stages.

Background

The company operates in a perishable goods FMCG environment and at the time had about 1,700 employees. It operated in six major categories, across four channels, plus export, and with eight manufacturing sites. They had a peak period which they called OND (October, November, December), and on average during the year, they processed about 50,000 orders a month.

The symptoms the company conveyed to us before we engaged with it was that customer service and delivery performance was down, inventory was up, costs were up, and the monthly S&OP (Integrated Business Planning) process just was not working—it had literally become paralyzed by analysis and backward-looking performance analysis.

It was now January, and the seasonal peak, which was now being called the OND crunch, was over. The focus was on making the ERP system work properly. Installation was only finished the October prior, and there was a collective wisdom gathering momentum that it was the new ERP system causing all the problems. Part of the issue was indeed that this implementation was on the tail end of a larger corporate project and the team was tired and the project was running late and over budget. The team had disbanded and moved on to other projects, roles, or even other companies, so a lot of the knowledge behind the setup walked out the door at the end of this project.

To add insult to injury, the ERP rollout was incomplete, consumed a huge amount of resources, and there was nothing left in the tank for the OND crunch. Digging deeper, we not only found that the company's Integrated Business Planning process had become paralyzed but also that its weekly replanning process had turned into an inventory write-off meeting. Oliver Wight was asked to do a diagnostic, and even in those early discussions, we started coaching the group to be more forward looking, but as the project lead for the engagement went on to say, "Every time we'd come up for air, another crisis hits us, and the first few new-style forward-looking meetings we tried, everyone would just boil over and erupt."

The other issue to surface was no one really understood the *end-to-end supply chain* or even information flow through their multiple channels and production facilities. There were a number of things missing and a number of processes being manage under the radar, such as critical steps missing from the production routings, storage locations that were invisible to the system and not widely known about, inflated capacity profiles, ad hoc inventory policy, a disconnect between marketing strategy and supply chain/operations capability, and more.

The company did, however, appoint a switched-on supply chain director the following May, just as we were starting to gain traction with the full transformation program, which helped elevate thinking enormously. There was also a cultural issue that was labeled the "nano-second culture," which meant if you could not get your point across in 3 seconds, people would walk away or leave the meeting. We did not believe this until we actually saw the CFO do that to someone. So, there were some value-eroding behaviors that also had to be addressed.

We did the diagnostic in March that year and presented to the executive team in early April . . . the clock was ticking for the business and the CEO. The CEO has had a long-term relationship with Oliver Wight and had been a successful CEO of the company for nearly 20 years. Even he said during the diagnostic, "I don't know how we got here; I don't know how to get out of it; and, I'm retiring in 6 months. Can we fix this in 6 months so I can go out on a high?" The answer was that it could not be fixed in 6 months, but with focus we could get a significant turnaround in that time. That really drove the motivation for getting things started quickly and effectively but also to deliver significant and sustainable quick wins.

Designing the Way Forward

The first piece of feedback to the executive team was that there is no silver bullet. We can still hear that collective groan of exasperation from the team when they heard that comment, made worse by the one that followed, which was, "This is a systemic problem . . .," which means there is no one core issue that, if fixed, will fix everything, ". . . it's systemic and it's endemic." Therefore the solutions lie in addressing the systemic nature of it, and the last statement in the headline to the executive team was, "There is a way forward . . . but it will require a radical change in the way you work . . . and time . . . and resources. Are you up for it?"

The question was then, how to get started and get some quick wins. We agreed to several principles and ground rules with the executive team that we could, and indeed did, keep referring back to:

- The ERP system is not the cause of the problem. We will actively reframe software discussion to the integrity of our processes. We will ensure people understand and follow the required behaviors before coming back to addressing issues with the ERP system.
- Each executive team member will take ownership of a planning and control process/discipline. That person will own the policy, the alignment of people's role descriptions to those policies, and hence appraise people's performance accordingly.
- Cross-functional teamwork and problem-solving will replace functional analysis and crisis management.
- The Pareto principle will be adopted in earnest.
- We must slow down to speed up, which translates to think small and safe, run pilots to test changes in a safe environment, learn from the pilots, apply the learning, and only then scale up.
- Investment in education for the executive team and people in the business, will take the highest priority.

The other practical agreement that was made was that while the executive team members were keen to focus on repairing their monthly Integrated Business Planning process, the speed to results was not going to happen through a monthly process. It was going to happen through their weekly replanning process. This was just simple math; a weekly cadence gives you 50+ opportunities a year for improving alignment of planning with execution, but the cadence of the monthly Integrated Business Planning process gives only 11+ improvement opportunities a year. This is not to say that elevating the Integrated Business Planning process was unimportant, it was just that Integrated Tactical Planning was going to give benefits quicker, albeit there needed to be a parallel improvement in the Integrated Business Planning process, because eventually the Integrated Tactical Planning process will need guidance and alignment with strategy.

The first task was to agree on where to start, and although we usually recommend piloting in a middle-of-the-road area that is not too hard and not too easy, this time we went for the pain point first, and instead of picking a category, a channel, or some other strip of the business, we settled on one critical SKU, because there was just too much noise going on to manage even a small number of SKUs. It was, however, an A SKU and critical to the business to get right. It was also following one of the guiding principles agreed by the executive team to "adopt in earnest" the Pareto principle.

Thereafter a cross-functional team of subject matter experts (SMEs) was formed who mapped the relevant end-to-end supply chain and then commenced a pilot Integrated Tactical Planning process as soon as the education was complete. Here are some of the early problem areas uncovered:

- The supply chain had never been mapped, and there was no one person who understood it end to end—there was no supply chain function at the time, and operations had little time to think of the bigger supply chain picture.
- There was no inventory policy beyond a few rudimentary and general rules, which had led to a proliferation of hundreds of unprofitable products.
- The ERP planning system was not well understood and the pilot needed to include how it worked end-to-end:
  - Execution process from order entry and promising to supplier purchase order release.
  - Planning processes from demand planning and forecasting to supplier management and improvement programs—everything was up for grabs.
- There was no effective control of master data accuracy and a separate team had to be set up to align the clunky, slow, and bureaucratic corporate requirements with a practical and quick turnaround solution for this division.
- Capacity planning turned out to be a major constraint to developing valid plans, because run rates were set to make the budget work, and there was no demonstrated capacity planning process to continually validate capability—they were setting themselves up to fail right from the annual planning processes.
- The marketing team had put a moratorium on launching new products for 6 months while the demand-and-supply planning processes were brought under control—for an FMCG business, that could have been a major catastrophe if it had continued too long.

Getting Traction—Moving from Reacting to Forward Looking

What they needed to do was focus on the important and urgent while also building all the other processes and linkages that were about longer-term capability and performance. As the integration lead said later, "The first few efforts were not pretty, and I know Oliver Wight would frown on this, but what we had to do was use the Integrated Tactical Planning process to fight the fires, while the Integrated Business Planning process was building the fire breaks."

Time was cleaved out to map the weekly process and weekly meeting. There was a lot of white paper around the room during the design session while people got their minds around moving from a shortage list focus, to a forward-looking planning mindset. The two specific areas that needed addressing urgently were the creation of valid plans using demonstrated capacity and focusing effort on effective root cause analysis for their customer delivery performance.

With respect to capacity, the company had to almost start from the beginning. The issue was that no one knew what the critical constraints were. Operations could describe critical machine and crewing limitations, and procurement could point to specific suppliers, and warehousing and logistics could point to storage and logistics, but because the end-to-end supply chain had never been mapped, and no data were collected, it was anyone's guess as to where the critical constraints were.

This led to spending time validating the numbers and setting up a process to routinely validate or adjust demonstrated capacity and *maximum demonstrated capacity* each month. The company started with machine throughput and quickly added warehouse and distribution capability because of the cost and limited refrigerated storage and transport that was required. There was also another behavioral shift required. They had been planning at 100% capacity, which was a double whammy because the capacity was not right in the first place; secondly, that left no room to be flexible when things went wrong. They removed both issues at once by starting to plan at about 95% of demonstrated capacity. This obviously made people really nervous. As the operations manager reflected some months later, "It was fascinating to watch; not only were we planning with significantly less capacity, counterintuitively, but it actually started to free up capacity, which we thought would have been impossible 6 months ago."

They then went on a campaign of getting the basics right:

- Publishing key measures focusing on, in the first instance, data metrics, for example, inventory record, material master, routings, and bills of material accuracy.
- Building a tight demand execution process to compare sales orders with the forecast every day.
- Building a culture of keeping to their customer promise, which was aligned with building a detailed inventory policy and clearly defining

the abnormal demand management process and change management notifications.

- Focusing on weekly plans out to the planning time fence and the variations week to week.
- Building the confidence in the organization for using the supply chain as a competitive advantage rather than an excuse.

After the first 4 weeks, the process started to hit its rhythm. In a big departure from what they had been doing, the integration lead started to collate critical information, starting with a scorecard. The scorecard was divided into four sections: demand, supply chain, production, and business. The demand section captured weekly demand variance and bias to forecast. The supply chain metrics started with inventory record accuracy, distribution performance, and supplier delivery performance. Production captured its master supply plan performance, manufacturing performance, and stability. The business metrics were customer delivery performance, days forward cover, and obsolescence.

As the process developed, the group started including more SKUs. They knew, however, that there were too many SKUs to publish and go through in a 45-minute weekly meeting, so the schedule was published for the next 2 weeks, and weekly rough-cut capacity planning graphs were used to highlight the validity (or otherwise) of the critical work centers. This was a great step forward, because although the detail was there underlying the capacity plans, the team didn't have to review it to understand whether plans were doable or not.

Week-by-week the information pack and supporting processes grew. A product road map was introduced early on to kick start the stalled product development process (see Figure 8.1), which turned out to be a major test of the process and almost fractured the newly forming process and discipline.

Project	Product	Wk0	Wk1	Wk2	Wk3	Wk4	Wk5	Wk6	Wk7	Wk8	Wk9	Wk10	Wk11	Wk12	Wk13
New1	Name1	■													
New2	Name2						■								
New3	Name3														■
New4	Name4			■											
New5	Name5						■								
New6	Name6								■						
New7	Name7											■			

FIGURE 8.1 Product Introduction Road Map

Source: Oliver Wight. Copyright Oliver Wight International, Inc. Used with permission.

The operations team, armed with their new demonstrated capacity planning process, pushed back, "We can't do it! There is absolutely no capacity left for anything new right now, even with pushing it to maximum demonstrated capacity for a few weeks. We should have seen this coming earlier. Maybe we can fit it in 4 months' time, after Christmas."

The marketing and sales team, however, were agitating strongly to just do it like they were used to doing. As an example of slowing down before speeding up, the quorum got together to explore options before just saying no, and then came back to the warring groups with several options and brokered an agreement. It was not particularly palatable to the marketing and sales team, but it excited the operations team. The plan was to stop making several C SKUs and agree to take a hit on customer service for 4 months and free up the capacity. As it turned out, those C SKUs were never made again, and there was no discernible drop in profitability . . . oh, and the new product was a massive success.

The lesson is that supply chain and operations should only use that no word sparingly, and only when everything else has been discounted. The answer should be "yes, but. . . ." The marketing and sales team must also resist using the old attitude of "just bang it into the schedule and make it work."

Once the key metrics started to be published, the next step was to start doing root cause analysis and developing corrective action plans. The company balked at doing that for every key metric, because, as they argued, "There is a lot of work in getting the data each week, and we're only just starting to get our systems to automate some of this; how about we just focus on customer delivery performance, which will kill two birds with the one stone, in that we'll be fixing a major issue for us right now, *and* it will uncover the other flow-through yield and data problems as part of the analysis."

Figure 8.2 was one of the earlier Pareto charts published and it did indeed point the way to a number of underlying process issues that led up to poor customer service.

Eventually the other rolled-through yield metrics were included in the root cause analysis, as well as inventory record accuracy for the Integrated Tactical Planning process. The flow-through yield metrics were supplier delivery, manufacturing (semifinished goods) schedule attainment, finished goods schedule attainment, and distribution performance, all in support of achieving greater than 95% customer service performance. The rationale for these was that if any are not performing at 95% minimum, then the whole chain of events breaks down, as the following table demonstrated.

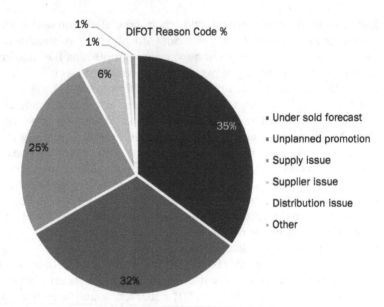

FIGURE 8.2 Reason Code Analysis for Misses in Customer Delivery Performance (DIFOT)

Source: Oliver Wight. Copyright Oliver Wight International, Inc. Used with permission.

Examples	Supplier (S)	Manufac- turing (M)	Finished Goods (FG)	Distribu- tion (D)	DIFOT (delivered in full on time) (CS)	Rolled- Through Yield = S × M × FG × D × CS
Best performers	99%	99%	99%	99%	99%	95.1%
Minimum expectations	95%	95%	95%	95%	95%	77.4%
One node not performing	95%	95%	95%	80%	95%	65.2%
Mediocre results	85%	85%	85%	85%	85%	44.4%

So, although Oliver Wight's Phase 1 target is a minimum of 95% at each point, the rolled-through yield is only 77.4%, which means there is still greater than 22% waste in that system. That waste could be defined as overproduction, waiting, quality issues and rejects, rework, safety stock and just-in-case inventory holding, long production runs, long lead times, and many more issues. As the table shows, at 99% there is very little waste in that supply chain.

You are probably asking, "Where did the 95% come from then?" The reason for 95% as the first step was a target used by the real Oliver Wight in his early consulting days, and he used it because he said, "At this point, the planning system will work fine, and there will be only the occasional data or process issues to adjust. Drop below 95%, however, and no one will use the planning system because it is just too corrupt."

There is also a counterargument we hear often: that there is a diminishing return on effort to achieve and keep performance any higher than 95%. Indeed, some operations people in Company X argued strongly in the early days of the program that this diminishing return started at 90% customer delivery performance, and 92% was about the right level of cost versus customer satisfaction. Modern benchmarking evidence, however, clearly shows that companies who do consistently achieve high process and data performance (greater than 98%), do it at half the cost of the lesser performers. So, not only does high data and process performance drive better customer satisfaction and employee satisfaction but also it is good for profitability.

At about this time, the data governance team was managing other data masters such as bills of material, routings, and item (material) masters, and as they went from piloting to routine audits the accuracy on those were routinely achieving accuracy approaching 100%.

One of the later additions to the process was to manage the execution of the whole product portfolio plans (see the following table).

Product	Last Order Date	Last Production Date	Expected Write-off Costs
SKU ITEM 1	31 Mar	25 Mar	$5,000
SKU ITEM 2	31 Mar	26 Mar	$3,000

The introduction of the phase-out plans to the Integrated Tactical Planning process corresponded with the creation and deployment of a detailed inventory policy, which among other things, covered A, B, C classification, as well as D-for-delete. If a SKU met certain criteria, the product portfolio management process had to put it up for deletion and could only keep it if there was a strategic justification. The following are the primary criteria that defined a D SKU:

- Annual projected volume below x tons.
- Margin below y%.

- No growth projected in the forecast.
- Not a companion sale to a major SKU.
- Not part of a range of SKUs.
- Not a new product.

The company also toyed with a one-in, one-out rule, which many companies have adopted, but settled for setting an ideal number of SKUs under the current manufacturing footprints as a target, which was included in their supply review scorecard.

Results 12 Weeks On

The focus on customer service had an immediate impact on case fill, with DIFOT (delivered in full on time) taking a little longer to close the gap (see Figure 8.3).

Customer Delivery Performance

The difference between case fill and DIFOT is that case fill measures just the volume of products being delivered, and the type of product is not considered. DIFOT, however, measures the delivery as the right SKU, in the right volume, and on time. By way of example, one beverage company

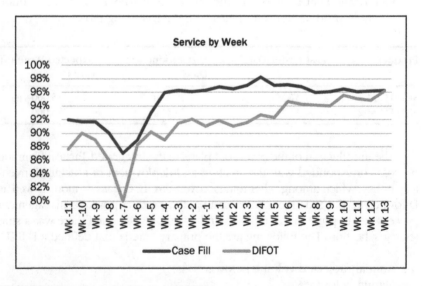

FIGURE 8.3 Weekly Case Fill and DIFOT

we worked with would quite often substitute a 2-liter beverage for a 1-liter order if they were running short of the 1-liter product and think that was okay and scored a hit on their delivery measure. A DIFOT metric would have scored that a miss on SKU and volume.

In Company X's case, the reason it took a little longer to narrow the gap between DIFOT and case fill was not the obvious one. A SKU- and time-based metric is harder to achieve than a pure volume metric, but the real reason in this case was their traditional data management and perceptions.

Case fill was their traditional metric and there were a few old hands who could not easily shake their affinity to it. One of the arguments was that their customers used case fill as their supplier performance metric and as long as they hit 92%, "Everyone was happy." There were three problems with this argument:

- The customer might have agreed to this many decades ago, but in this modern and very competitive world, the grocery channel, especially, is now expecting a minimum of 98% delivered in full, by SKU, on time, within a time slot of 2 hours.
- Case fill is a gross measure and hides myriad sins at a detail level—without a SKU- and time-based measure, there is not enough detail to effective do root cause analysis.
- The sales history of these SKUs then become the history that is used in the forecasting system, and without a rigorous data maintenance process to clean up sales history, it will cause erroneous statistical forecasts.

There were of course, data accuracy issues to fix, which took some time, and there were multiple systems being used with different units-of-measure definitions and different reporting cut-off times, all of which needed the due diligence done to align the data and tighten the timing.

There was one final piece of the puzzle that baffled us at Oliver Wight and the company's Integrated Tactical Planning team. Although this might sound like a one-off issue for this company, we have found that this occurs much more often than one would have guessed. The story went like this—and bear with it, because it was not too logical and had a lot of emotions. A new supply chain and operations director started several weeks into the program and resurrected the case fill argument once again, trotting out the same argument that the trade were just fine with 92% case fill performance because that is how they measure our performance. The team thought that it would be good to approach a sample of customers and verify it once and for all. As expected, the trade had moved on and were in fact measuring both case fill and supplier DIFOT, but only talked case fill because they thought that that was the only language Company X understood.

The supply chain and operations director came back later and said that the problem was solved because the case fill measure was actually captured at the SKU level. That was partially true because some of the systems were set up for SKU-based measurements, but most were not. That set off a small project to align the reporting systems, but the supply chain and operations director had one final curve ball, which would have been funny had the situation not been so heated.

He made a comment during an Oliver Wight debriefing session that "We should be aiming for 85% case fill anyway because that allows us to be more flexible." At that point the CEO stood up and said, "DIFOT is a business measure, owned by all of us in the leadership team, and we need to be held accountable to consistently hitting a minimum of 95%."

At least at that point the argument was over and the team could move on. The reason we went into a little more detail about this story is that even a simple change in metrics must be seen as a change management activity. We were not only changing the calculation and process of data capture, but also we were changing some very deep-seated paradigms that can't be easily changed even with compelling logic and data. It is not that people are naturally opposed to change, but most people have enough to do in their day-to-day world, and change can be seen as just adding more work. When overtly challenging stated positions and long-held beliefs, we need to recognize that there will be resistance and plan the change journey accordingly.

Inventory and Obsolescence

Inventory and obsolescence reductions were stunning results (see Figure 8.4). In only 12 weeks since kicking off the Integrated Tactical Planning process, the company saw a paradoxical result of the paper level of overall capacity decline by 15%, inventory volume reduction of 10%, inventory

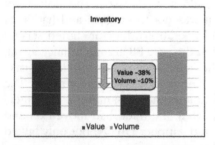 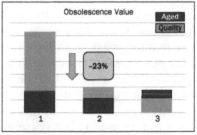

FIGURE 8.4 Inventory and Obsolescence 12 Weeks On

value reduction of 38%, obsolescence decline by 23%, and DIFOT maintained over 96%. This continued for many months thereafter, and although it may seem counterintuitive on the surface, this is a typical scenario we see time and time again.

What Would They Have Done Differently?

As the company was preparing for its project-closure presentation, there were two questions they need to reflect on:

- What would you have done differently?
- What are the continuous improvement plans from here on?

With regards to doing things differently, the team came up with six gold standards, which will be a suitable way to conclude the chapter and the book.

IT IS A JOURNEY

As the integration lead commented on the whole program, "When I was appointed project lead, I thought it was just a project, but as our Oliver Wight consultants keep saying, this is a change journey, so let's set it up for success and sustainability; he was right."

As mentioned previously, with respect to changing the thinking about and calculation for DIFOT, if something so simple and logical can tie people in knots, then don't underestimate the challenges you will face during a full program of work, but don't let that put you off. Once complete, the results can be stunning, and not just for the performance metrics and goals. As one company reported recently, "Our internal climate survey jumped from a respectable 3.8 out of 5, to 4.4. People really like working in environments like this."

BEST PRACTICE DOES NOT JUST RUB OFF

Once the team had commenced the live pilot, they genericized the templates, agendas, metrics, and policies and shared them with the next category due to start, but it turned out to be a false start. The next category did not jump at the chance and didn't see that this was going to improve the way they worked, even though the results were there for everyone to see. As the head of that category said later, "People just don't absorb this stuff like osmosis. We had to go back to first principles of change management and deploy the education, engage people in designing the process to suit their category (while staying true to the fundamental principles and concepts). We also had to acknowledge the differences to the first category and be prepared to adapt appropriately."

Every one of the rollouts were different, and each its share of hurdles and paradigm shifts to be managed, but it did get easier each time because the team was on the watch for where and when potential obstacles would occur.

There is also a waning of discipline that occurs over time. As the team rolled the process out to all the categories, they found they needed to come back to the earlier processes because they'd lost focus over time. This is mostly because the drive for continuous improvement hadn't been embedded, but it is also just human nature. People get comfortable with a certain way of working but then tend to tolerate a slow erosion of discipline over time because they seem to be managing okay without the extra checks and balances. They learn to expect the unexpected, and over time it becomes normal practice. . . which simply means people get used to work-arounds and just fixing things as they occur. The learning is that there needs to be a framework of continuous improvement that people buy in to and share the same passion for a never-ending flow of improvements, which the Japanese call *Gemba Kaizen*—take a walk to where the value is created and continuously improve it.

CHANGE AGENTS ARE GOLD

There is an old saying, "One person trying to create a change will fail; two people trying to create a change can at least commiserate with each other when they do fail; but when three people try to create a change, it is the beginning of a full-scale revolution."

In this context the program tapped into a number of people who wanted to make change, and they were chosen for the integration team and led elements of the program as it matured. Similarly, there were three people on the executive team who were also leading the charge. As elements of the program were completed, these people were reassigned to lead or participate in other teams to share their experience, which created a kind of snowball effect.

This was highlighted through the number of people changes that occurred during the program. Just before the integration lead moved onto another role, he commented, "We are onto our third CEO, second marketing director, third supply chain director, second CFO, and we're still going. It's because there were people on the team who believed in this, and when they were asked to lead an element, they didn't have to be told what to do or constantly supported; they just got on with it and reported on progress." At times, the integration lead and integration team are chosen because they are "not so busy." This is the wrong reason for choosing people. It is vital that people are chosen because they are self-starters, can influence others, and believe in the vision. Before starting a change journey, it is worth mapping out the key influencers across the organization to ensure the right people are driving the change. Influencers can come from any part of the organization and at any level. Combining those people with an executive team leading the change can save a lot of time in building momentum and reducing the anxiety that always accompanies the early days of change.

DON'T SKIMP ON RESOURCES, EDUCATION, OR CONTINUOUS COMMUNICATION

The HR delegate to the team was a little confused as to what her role was in the beginning, saying, "I really don't understand all this technical stuff, so what am I doing here?" Within a matter of weeks, she understood. It is all too easy to agree to allocation of resources, but then actually getting them and managing them is a whole different question.

She said later, "When we did the pilot, we did everything by the book, but once we started to roll out to the broader organization, we got a little blasé and thought that after such great results with the pilot, everyone would willingly come on board, but that was not the case. We needed to make sure the education was done for everyone, a team was appointed, and space allowed for them to fully understand the expectations, and we even resurrected and rolled out the original communication plan. It made a huge difference. People just know when you're genuinely showing an interest in them . . . or not!"

Although the mechanics might be the same with each rollout—for example, process steps, the formats and templates, and the metrics—the important thing to remember is that people will be at all different levels of understanding and engagement, so the change management program for the rollouts needs to be just as rigorous as it was for the pilots.

CHOOSE THE IMPLEMENTATION PACE WISELY

The CEO made the comment in the beginning that the company didn't treat the original ERP installation with the respect it warranted, and hence they found themselves in nowhere land. He asked Oliver Wight how we would recommend they approach this program, and we suggested two strategies:

- A traditional approach, which follows a path from education, to process design, offline piloting, and a series of progressively bigger live pilots that allows time for people to come on the journey with you—sometimes referred to a slow-infiltration approach.
- Similar to the traditional approach, but in this case the go-live step is when everything is done all at once—sometimes referred to as the big bang when it is not done well or rapid deployment approach if it is effectively planned and executed.

The original ERP installation was a big bang approach, and it skimped on the education, the people engagement plan, and allowing enough time in piloting. In this case people were gun-shy, and the agreement was that the Integrated Tactical Planning process would use the first approach, but focus on the area of greatest difficulty and greatest need. It does take longer to get to full go live but once there it is more embedded and sustainable, and there is much less rework than if you go big bang without the requisite prework.

This doesn't mean a rapid deployment approach can't work—it is about choosing wisely and that means assessing the risk versus effort. In a subsequent demand management and forecasting program, the sales SME chose the rapid deployment approach with great success. She said afterwards, "That was a great approach, but you were right about planning it well; formally we did six offline pilots, but there were numerous user tests and we consulted with dozens of people before having our go-live conference."

TRANSLATE WINS INTO SUSTAINABLE OUTCOMES

This is related to the mentioned communication plan, but is worth pulling out separately, because it is the content part of the communication plan. There is a misperception that you need to be a creative genius to keep up appropriate communication, but in reality, content is everywhere if you look at it the right way.

Every event is an opportunity to communicate a win or a learning. In the start-up phase there are results from the diagnostic, announcements about dates, content for education or process design workshops, then dry runs, piloting, and go live. Each win then builds the definitions for people and behavior, process design evolution, and improvements in system application to facilitate better process adherence. Even when something doesn't go to plan, the learnings are often very significant, and sharing these can be invaluable in showing transparency and honesty.

Once the weekly routine is established, a typical communiqué is to publish a one-pager that summarizes the changes, the decisions made, the updated plans, and the continuous improvement initiatives, which should be shared with appropriate people.

In the case of Company X, the integration lead even developed an entertaining weekly blog that reach many hundreds of people, both inside her division and the wider global organization and beyond. When asked how she managed to find the time and creativity to do that, she said, "Every time I write an article, I say the same thing—I'm not going to be able to do that again next week—but by the time I get to next week, if I've kept my eyes open, there is always something to talk about. I even wrote a blog on the disagreement with how DIFOT was measured, and it turned into an opportunity to talk about the process of root cause analysis and how almost all root causes eventually end up as a process issue."

Conclusion

So, with those parting words from the Integration Lead, this brings us to the end of the book. We have covered a lot of ground to get here: from the rationale for Integrated Tactical Planning, to its alignment with the Integrated Business Planning process, to the elements of the process, to managing the change journey, and to finishing with a case study.

This has been a wonderful journey for the Oliver Wight team—Rod Hozack, Stuart Harman, Todd Ferguson, and Dawn Howarth—and we look forward to hearing about your journeys in mastering the art of process management. As Oliver Wight consultants we love what we do. We are keen to share what we know and what we have experienced, and we are also keen to continue to learn, write about it, and share our learnings, such as defined in our definition of excellence, *The Oliver Wight Class A Standard for Business Excellence*, 7th ed. (2017).

Special thanks should also go to our Oliver Wight colleagues and Oliver Wight the man. Without the core principles that Oliver Wight so generously shared with us while we were in industry, and the collective experiences of all the Oliver Wight Associates from around the world, we would not have been able to have written this book.

Good luck, and remember, if you do not try, you will not succeed.

Glossary of Terms

ABC Classification   A method of categorizing items based on dollar value, volume, or other criteria. The A items are those with the greatest dollar impact and hence receive the most attention in terms of control. B items have less dollar impact and receive less control effort, and the C items have the least impact of all. *See* Pareto Principle.

Abnormal Demand   A demand that is not part of the forecast. Typically, an abnormal demand is a large, one-time order.

Above the Line   Aggregate planning.

Accountability   Refers to the role that owns a metric or KPI. *See also* Policy and Procedures.

Action Messages   Outputs of an MRP system that identify the need for and the type of actions to be taken to correct a current or a potential demand-supply-inventory imbalance. Examples of action messages are "Release Order," "Reschedule Out," and "Cancel." *Also known as* Exception Messages and Alerts.

Activity-Based Costing (ABC)   A method of cost accounting in which overhead is applied to products by means of "cost drivers," which are those elements that directly cause costs. This is in contrast to traditional methods of product costing, which often allocate overhead via a relatively unrelated factor such as direct labor hours. For example, product engineering overhead may be more accurately allocated to products based on the number of design changes per product, rather than via direct labor hours.

Aggregate Business Planning   The process of comparing the sales forecast to the supply capabilities to develop a business strategy that includes a supply plan, budgets and financial statements, and supporting plans for purchasing, workforce, technical, and other plans.

Anticipated Delay Report   A report issued by the next step in the supply chain to advise that supply might be late or short. This is an essential ingredient of a closed-loop planning system.

Assumptions   Careful records of the criteria used to generate strategies, business plans, budgets, forecasts, supply plans, and so on, so that if challenged in the future, the reasoning behind a particular plan can still be understood, even if the originator is no longer available.

Available-to-Promise (ATP) The uncommitted portion of a company's inventory or planned production. This figure is usually calculated from the master production schedule and is maintained as a tool for order promising.

Below the Line Detailed planning and scheduling.

Bias A phenomenon in which plans are developed that continually understate or overstate a situation. An example might be when sales understate the forecast in order to achieve a better performance bonus at the end of the year.

Bill of Material *See* Master Data.

Bow Wave The effect created on the master schedule when requirements are balanced against capability in the short term, for example, the next 2 weeks, and all other requirements are pushed to outside the next 2 weeks, and unlikely to ever be caught up. The impact is an invalid master supply schedule and a never-ending pushing out of requirements.

Budget The first year of the business plan (*see* Business Plan for further information).

Business Plan A statement of business plans (usually 2 to 3 years), income projections, costs, and profits, usually accompanied by budgets, a projected balance sheet, and a cash flow (source and application of funds) showing how the strategy will be implemented and deployed.

The standard 12-month window representing the company's commitments for its fiscal year and that supports the business plan requirements (often called the budget or annual operating plan [AOP]).

Capacity Requirements Planning (CRP) The process of determining how much labor, machine time, storage space, supplier capacity, transport routing, and other critical work areas are required to accomplish the tasks of supply plans. Includes the resolution of imbalances between demand for the resources and the demonstrated availability.

Change Control A formal process that is to be used for requesting and managing changes to products, processes, and policies to ensure changes are made with the knowledge and involvement of the appropriate people.

For the change control process to work effectively the rules associated with change and how to use the Change Control process must be understood. In addition, the authorization process needs to be clearly understood.

Class A A standard of business excellence as defined by the *Oliver Wight Class A Standard for Business Excellence* (7th ed.) and a program of improvements validated and accredited by Oliver Wight.

Cognitive Bias/Logical Fallacy A set of human heuristics that enable people to quickly sum up a situation and make a judgment on a course of action.

These heuristics, however, can be prone to misperception and cloud decision-making. An example of a logical fallacy is, "The warehouse is full; therefore, we have too much stock." or "If you shoot for the moon, you might land on Everest." An example of a cognitive bias is "I create great plans; it's just that operations doesn't want to stick to the plan." Or "My marketing plan is fantastic; it's just that sales doesn't think like a marketer and therefore can't follow it." Both are examples of attribution bias.

Contingency Planning   The concept that plans should be drawn up and held in reserve should the plans or strategic direction fail.

Core Plans   The three core plans are the product portfolio plan, the demand plan, and supply plan. All other plans are resultant from these plans; for example, inventory is a resultant of the interplay between demand and supply plans and financial plans are outcomes of valuing the revenue of the product and demand plans, minus the direct cost of the supply plan and indirect costs and operating expenses expended to deliver the core plans.

Corrective-Action Plan   The plan identifying the steps needed to rectify a problem when it has been identified.

Cumulative Lead Time   The longest length of time involved to accomplish the activity in question. For any item planned through supply, it is found by reviewing each path through the supply chain and whichever adds up to the greatest number defines cumulative lead time. Also called aggregate lead time, stacked lead time, composite lead time, and critical path lead time.

Customer Promise   The result of analyzing and segmenting customers based on strategic importance and value to the business. The Customer Promise will then be composed of an optimal and competitive mix of parameters, such as lead times/availability, lot sizing, and delivery charges per segment.

Decision Points   Points in time in the future when decisions need to be made to satisfy current planning capability. For example, a material or finished goods might have a lead time to order of 3 months; therefore, the requirements for use of that material or finished goods needs to be agreed at least 3 months prior to having a product to ship or sell.

Demand   A need for a product or component that could come from any number of sources: customer order, forecast, interplant, branch warehouse, service part, or to manufacture the next higher level. *See* Dependent Demand, Independent Demand.

Demand Execution   A process for matching sales orders to the forecast. This should be at least weekly and, depending on industry and product type, is typically daily and sometimes hourly.

Demand Management   The process and series of techniques for planning and forecasting future demand on the business.

Demand Manager The role of managing the integrity of the end-to-end demand planning and forecasting process. Also called Demand Planner, Execution Manager.

Demand Monitoring *See* Demand Execution.

Demand Plan The set of activities and drivers that need to be actioned to deliver the forecast numbers.

Demonstrated Capacity Capacity calculated from actual performance data. It is a concept that uses realistic plans to plan supply, without top-down expectations and unrealistic stretch goals.

Demonstrated Performance The performance actually being achieved. The difference between demonstrated performance and available theoretical capacity is known as the load factor or efficiency factor and is used to calculate the planned demonstrated performance.

Demand Review/Demand Plan Demand Review is a monthly meeting focused on agreeing an unconstrained demand plan over a horizon of 24 to 36 months. It is an integral element of the Integrated Business Planning process.

Dependent Demand When demand comes from planned resupply for the next step in the supply chain, such as a material component of a finished product. These demands should be calculated, not forecasted. A given item may have both dependent and independent demand at any given time.

Delivery In Full, On Time (DIFOT) A customer service metric that measures being delivered in full and on time to a customer order.

Distribution Center A warehouse with finished goods and/or service items made elsewhere. A company, for example, might have a manufacturing facility in Philadelphia and distribution centers in Atlanta, Dallas, Los Angeles, San Francisco, and Chicago. The term *distribution center* is synonymous with the term *branch warehouse,* although the former has become more commonly used. When there is a warehouse that regularly supplies other warehouses, it may be called a *regional distribution center.*

Distribution Network The system that has been created to distribute products to the customers and consumers.

Distribution Requirements Planning (DRP) The function of determining the need to replenish inventory at distribution centers. The planned orders at the distribution center level are "exploded" via DRP to become gross requirements on the supplying source. In the case of multilevel distribution networks, this explosion process can continue down through the various levels of a regional distribution center, factory warehouse, and any other steps before the master supply schedule. Demand on the supplying source(s) is recognized as dependent. Distribution Resource Planning is the extension of DRP into the planning of the key resources contained in a distribution system, such as warehouse space, manpower, money, trucks, and freight cars.

Dynamic Data   A term used to describe data that change as a result of ongoing business transactions, such as inventory movement, as opposed to static data, which is data that are changed only as the rules of the business change, such as batch quantities or bill of materials. *See also* Master Data.

Engineer to Order (ETO)   Products in which the customer specifications require unique engineering design, significant customization, or new purchased materials. Each customer order results in a unique set of part numbers, bills of materials, and routings.

Enterprise Resource Planning (ERP)   A computer system that allows the business to plan, integrate, and manage a business across multiple sites and operations in a seamless manner. It obviates the need to order between these entities and supply chain steps.

Escalation Criteria   Criteria designed to empower frontline workers to make decisions until a certain set of conditions arise, at which point there is a defined process for escalating decisions to a group higher up in the organization.

Exception Messages and Alerts   *See* Action Messages.

FMCG   Fast-moving consumer goods.

Focus Month   Defined as the first month outside cumulative lead time (CLT). For example, if the CLT is 3 months, then the focus month is month 4 into the future. This is used to signal the importance of getting the demand plan as good as it can be in preparation for placing purchase orders to fulfill requirements for 3 months hence.

Forecast Consumption   The process of consuming the forecast as customer orders are entered. The sum of the unconsumed forecast and the booked customers should remain constant unless an intentional change to the forecast is desired. Abnormal demands should not consume the forecast.

Forecast Roll   Unconsumed forecast can be rolled into the next period providing there have been no changes to assumptions. At the end of a month the decision to roll may be changed because the next month forecast should not be increased if the assumptions have not been changed; in this case it could be dropped.

Funnel   The stage-and-gate process for managing new product introductions is often referred to as a funnel in that projects should be eliminated at each stage to ensure fewer, but more effective, products are launched. When graphically displayed, it should look like a funnel.

Gates   *See* Stage-and-Gate Process.

Horizon   The time covered by future planning, for example, for the Integrated Business Planning process it is typically 24 to 36 months, and for the Integrated Tactical Planning process it is usually about 13 weeks.

Independent Demand   When such demand is unrelated to the demand for other items. Demand for finished goods and service parts are examples of independent demand if they are from customers.

Integrated Business Model   A comprehensive set of best-practice processes, designed to integrate the business across nine business elements: Strategic Planning, People and Teams, Continuous Improvement, Integrated Business Planning, Product Management, Demand Management, Supply Chain Management, Internal Supply Management, and External Supply Management.

Integrated Business Planning   A monthly management process comprising five key elements: Product Management Review, Demand Review, Supply Review, Reconciliation Review, and Management Business Review.

Integrated Tactical Planning   A weekly cross-functional replanning process designed to ensure the business stays on track to deliver the first 3 months of the signed-off Integrated Business Planning process plans, thereby releasing time for senior management to spend on strategy.

Inventory Policy   A critical business policy that defines how the business will manage inventory and includes elements such as SKU classification, SKU rationalization, the volume and value of safety stock, and the physical parameters for planning, for example, lead times and lot sizes.

Item/Material Master   The master record for an item. Typically, it contains identifying and descriptive data, planning values (such as lead times and order quantities), and may contain data on inventory status, requirements, and planned orders. Item records are linked together by bill of material records (or product structure records), thus defining the bill of material.

Lead Time   A span of time required to perform an activity, usually the procurement of materials and/or products either from an outside supplier or from one's own manufacturing facility. The individual components of any given lead time can include some or all the following: order preparation time, queue time, set-up time, production time, move or transportation time, receiving and inspection time.

Lead-Time Offset   A term used in MRP when a planned order receipt in one time period will require the release of that order in some earlier time period based on the lead time for the item. The difference between the due date and the release date is the lead-time offset.

Lean   Lean is a methodology to be applied when flow can be established and supply achieved against a pull from demand. The methodology follows five steps to the perfect Lean enterprise. Lean is the antidote to waste (MUDA). It is a way to do more and more with less and less— less human effort, less equipment, less time, less space—while coming closer to providing customers exactly what they want. A way of creating work rather than simply destroying jobs in the name of efficiency.

Load The amount of work scheduled for a manufacturing facility, usually expressed in standard hours, or units of production.

Load Profile A statement of the key resources required to manufacture one unit of a selected item. Often used to predict the impact of the item scheduled in the production plan and/or the master supply schedule on these resources. Also called Resource Profile.

Logical Fallacy *See* Cognitive Bias/Logical Fallacy.

Make to Order Frequently, long lead time components are planned prior to the customer order arriving to reduce the delivery time to the customer. A make-to-order product for which key components (bulk, semifinished, intermediate, subassembly, fabricated, purchased, and packaging) used in the assembly or finishing process are planned and stocked in anticipation of a customer order.

Make to Stock A product planned to be shipped routinely from finished goods, off-the-shelf, and therefore finished prior to the customer order being placed.

Management by Exception A principle in management in which management decisions that cannot be made at one level are passed up to the next level for a decision. The principle used in budgetary control in which items of income or expenditure that show no variance or small variances require no action, whereas exceptional items showing adverse variances to an unacceptable level require action to be taken.

It is also a technique to highlight the changes to plans since the last time the plan was updated. In the Integrated Business Planning process, this would be a comparison of the plans signed off last month to the current plans that have resulted from adding an extra month of actual results and an extra month to the rolling projections. In the Integrated Tactical Planning process, it is a similar concept, except the comparison is to the plans agreed last week, with the new plans this week.

Master Data The data that are being used in a planning system to manage the business through the system in a formal manner. Examples of common master data are bills of material, routings, work-center files, and item (material) master.

Master Planning and Scheduling The anticipated build schedule. The master supply planner maintains this schedule and, in turn, it becomes a set of planning numbers that drives MRP. It represents what the company plans to produce expressed in specific configurations, quantities, and dates. The master supply schedule must take into account customer orders and forecasts, backlog, availability of material, availability of capacity, and management policy and goals.

Master Supply Planner/Scheduler The role of managing the integrity of the end-to-end supply planning and scheduling process across a site and/or supply chain.

Material Requirements Planning (MRP) A set of techniques that uses bills of material, inventory data, and the master production schedule to calculate requirements for items. It makes recommendations to release replenishment orders for material. Further, because it is time-phased, it makes recommendations to reschedule open orders when due dates and need dates are not in phase. Originally seen as merely a better way to order inventory, today it is thought of as primarily a scheduling technique, that is, a method for establishing and maintaining valid due dates on orders. It is the foundation for closed-loop MRP.

Maturity Chart A methodology that assesses a company's level of business sophistication based on a series of four phases from being disconnected in Phase 1, to everything being integrated in Phase 4.

Maximum Demonstrated Capacity The planned demonstrated capacity increased by a known achievable amount, such as authorization of overtime or adding a shift, but without expending capital. This is usually doable for a short period of time but is not sustainable in the longer term.

New Product Introduction (NPI) New product introduction defines processes for creating and introducing a new product or new service that the firm has not marketed previously. It usually excludes products or services that are minor modifications, line extensions, or only changed in promotions.

Node A step in a supply chain, for example, a warehouse, manufacturing site, or retail outlet, usually outside the immediate company's supply chain.

Normal-Cause Variation A range of variation around a forecast number that is consistently variable and poses no material impact on planning parameters. Applies to selling more than forecasting. Typically managed through safety parameters, such as safety stock, lead-time offset, lead times, and safety materials. When selling less than forecast, this is typically managed through reserve warehouses space, multiskilling, and flexible manufacturing resources.

Opportunity An upside to a plan that is not currently in the plan and is dependent on a set of circumstances occurring that is usually outside the company's ability to create or has a higher-than-acceptable degree of uncertainty associated.

Optimization The action of making the best of something; the state or the condition of being optimal to ensure the most cost-effective supply of product and/or service. It is usually supported by a series of simulations to derive the best outcome via manipulating input variables, such as cost, delivery, quality, and distribution.

Order Entry   The process of accepting and translating what a customer wants into terms used by the supplier company. This can be as simple as creating shipping documents for a finished goods product to a far more complicated series of activities including engineering effort for engineer-to-order products.

Order Point   An inventory replenishment technique that considers forecasted demand over replenishment lead time, plus an allowance for safety stock. When the available inventory of an item drops below the order point, a replenishment order is triggered. This technique assumes that demand is linear and consistent and as such is not appropriate for virtually all items with dependent demand. The "two-bin," "min-max," and "order-up-to" techniques are all variations of the basic order point approach, and they are considered short-term "execution" techniques that need a longer-range planning process sitting over the top to give direction.

Order Promising   The process of making a delivery commitment that is answering the question, "When can you ship?" For make-to-order products this usually involves a check of material and capacity availability and the promise of a delivery date. This can be greatly facilitated via the use of available-to-promise information in the master schedule.

Pareto Principle   The Pareto Principle is known by a number of other terms, such as the "Law of the Vital Few" and the "Law of the Trivial Many." For example, in many companies 30% to 60% of the sales come from 5% to 10% of the products. It is the basis for ABC inventory analysis and classification and is used extensively within Just-In-Time and Total Quality Control.

Past-Due Orders   Orders in the planning system with a past-due completion date. Past-due orders can drive erroneous plans and need to be corrected to a future date or deleted.

Planned Demonstrated Capacity   Shop floor commitment of hours available to the planner for scheduling purposes that will be based on the demonstrated capacity; consequently, it is often referred to as planned demonstrated capacity. It is the expected capacity to be available in a future time period.

Planned Order   A suggested order quantity and due date created by an MRP planning system processing when it encounters net requirements. Created by the computer; exists only within the computer and may be changed or deleted by the computer during subsequent MRP processing if conditions change. Planned orders at one level will be exploded into gross requirements for components at the next lower level. Planned orders also serve as input to capacity requirements planning, along with scheduled receipts, to show the total capacity requirements in future time periods.

Policy and Procedures   Documents describing a process and controlled by a formal document-control process. The policy part defines the rules of the process and includes roles, responsibilities, and accountabilities; is owned by a senior executive; and is signed off by the lead team, at least annually. The procedure part is usually supported by process-flow charts and is a detailed, step-by-step description of how the process works.

Postlaunch Review   A formal process designed to assess the effectiveness of bringing new products to market and embedding the learnings into the process.

Product Life Cycle Management and Assessment   Refers to the management and assessment of products as they move through the stages of product life, from development and introduction, to growth, to maturity/stability, and finally to end of life.

Product Management Review   A monthly meeting focused on agreeing the product portfolio plan over a horizon of 24 to 36 months. It is an integral element of the Integrated Business Planning process.

Product Portfolio Management   A business management practice that helps managers assess the product portfolio performance now and relative to a future position.

Product Project Manager   The role of managing the integrity of the end-to-end product portfolio management processes, and is often one of the quorum responsible for managing the Integrated Tactical Planning process.

Quorum   Key roles within a process, for example, the quorum for the Integrated Tactical Planning process are the product projects manager, the demand execution manager, the master supply scheduler, and order entry and promising.

Required Capacity   The capacity of a system or resource needed to produce a desired output in a particular time period.

Resource Profile   *See* Load Profile.

Root Cause Analysis   Finding the real cause of the problem and dealing with it rather than simply continuing to deal with the symptoms.

Rough-Cut Capacity Planning   The process of converting the production plan and/or the master supply plan into capacity needs for key resources: manpower, machinery, warehouse space, vendor capabilities, and in some cases, money. Load profiles are often used to accomplish this. The purpose of rough-cut capacity planning is to evaluate the plan prior to exploding it through MRP. Sometimes called resource requirements planning.

Routing   Information detailing the method of manufacture of a particular item that includes the operations to be performed, their sequence, the various work centers to be involved, and the standards for set up and run. In some companies, the routing also includes information on tooling, operator skill levels, inspection operations, and testing requirements.

Safety Stock In general, a quantity of stock planned to be available to protect against fluctuations in demand and/or supply.

Safety Time A technique in MRP whereby material is planned to arrive ahead of the requirement date. The difference between the requirement date and the planned in-stock-date is safety time.

Scenario Planning This is where the operational data in the planning systems is used to perform what-if evaluations of alternative plans to answer questions about the level of uncertainty. For conditions of high impact and high uncertainty, contingency plans should be developed and an assessment made of the trigger points for enacting the contingency plans.

Stage-and-Gate Process A methodology for bringing new products to market in a series of stages—doing the analytical and development work—and gates—where projects are matched again "must-meet" and "should-meet" criteria for a "go" or "kill" decision.

Static Data Data that remain relatively stable over time and are used to set up the planning system, for example, routings, bills of material, item (material) masters, and work-center files.

Stock-Keeping Units (SKUs) The primary items that a company makes or buys.

Strategic Initiatives Activities that have resulted, or will result, from the company's Strategic Planning Process. To achieve a company's 5- or 10-year strategic plan requires the prioritization of strategic initiatives to enable the company's future to be achieved.

Supply Chain A description of the movement of raw materials to the ultimate consumption of the finished products linking across supplier-user companies. The functions within and outside a company that enable the value chain to make products and services to customers. A network of nodes between a company and its suppliers, and a company and its consumers designed to effectively produce and distribute specific products or services. The entities in the supply chain include producers, vendors, warehouses, transportation companies, distribution centers, and retailers.

Supply Planner/Scheduler The role of managing the integrity of a supply point or number of supply points, supply planning, and execution processes. Also referred to as master supply planner or master supply scheduler.

Supply Points Manufacturing sites and distribution centers inside the company's management.

Supply Review A monthly meeting focused on agreeing on the supply plan to cost-effectively support the demand requirements on the business over a horizon of 24 to 36 months. It is an integral element of the Integrated Business Planning process.

Sustainability Plan   A set of activities that embeds and stabilizes process changes in an organization. Principle components:

- Policies and Procedures managed though a document-control process.
- Ongoing Education and Training in core management processes.
- Formal and embedded Communication and Feedback mechanisms.
- Role Descriptions aligned with the Policies and Procedures.
- Performance Appraisals aligned with Role Descriptions.

Takt Time   Based on the German word that means "pace," the rate or pace of production is matched to the pace of customer sales. Used in Lean Manufacturing to align production time in linked manufacturing processes.

Time Fences   A point in time in which various restrictions or changes in operating procedures take place. For example, changes to the master supply plan can be accomplished easily beyond the cumulative lead time, whereas changes inside the cumulative lead time become increasingly more difficult, to a point where changes should be resisted. Time fences can be used to define these points.

Time Zones   Zones between time fences. Usually there are two: (1) the emergency zone and (2) the trading zone. The trading zone lies between the cumulative lead time and the emergency time fence; consequently, the emergency zone indicates the period when assets are being used to supply products.

Value Proposition   A clear statement of the tangible results/benefits a customer gets from using our products/services. It translates the market offering into a statement of the benefits a customer will derive from doing business with us. (Wiersema: "A good value proposition is one that convinces target customers to do business with your company, rather than the competition. It will articulate what essential bundle of benefits and experiences the customer can expect to get, with what trade-offs and at what cost, and how that combination is superior to other viable sources.")

Value Stream Mapping   A technique that helps companies understand the flow of material and information as a product or service makes its way through a value stream. A value stream map takes into account not only the activity of the product but also the management and information systems that support the basic process. This is especially helpful when working to reduce cycle time, because insights are gained into the decision-making flow in addition to the process flow. It is a Lean tool. The first step is to map the process, then above the map identify the information flow that enables the process to occur, and finally note the value-added time versus the elapsed time.

Velocity The ratio between the steps in a process that add value divided by the total elapsed time, expressed as a percentage. This simple equation can be applied to any process, anywhere at any time, and gives a very useful benchmark information for improvement. To use this successfully employees need to understand exactly what is value-adding activity and what is non-value-adding activity.

Vendor Scheduling (VS) Vendor scheduling is a technique that shares time-phased requirements with the vendor generated straight out of the MRP system. The horizon can be as far out as the MRP system is set up to plan.

Waste Any activity that does not add value to the product or service in the eyes of the customer or consumer. In other words, if an invoice was sent to a customer with all the supplier's activities listed, would the customer happily pay for them all? It is also the by-product of a process or task with unique characteristics requiring special management control.

Work Center One or more people and/or machines that can be considered as one unit for purposes of capacity planning and detailed scheduling.

References

Correll, J. G., & Herbert, K. (2007). *Gaining control: Managing capacity and priorities* (3rd. ed.). John Wiley & Sons, Inc.

Ling, R. C., & Goddard, W. E. (1988). *Orchestrating success: Improve control of the business with sales and operations planning.* John Wiley & Sons, Inc.

Oliver Wight International. (2017). *The Oliver Wight class a standard for business excellence* (7th ed.). John Wiley & Sons, Inc.

Proud, J. F. (2013). *Master scheduling: A practical guide to competitive manufacturing* (3rd. ed.). John Wiley & Sons Inc.

Schorr, J. E. (1998). *Purchasing in the 21st century.* John Wiley & Sons, Inc.

Wight, O. W. (1981). *Manufacturing resource planning: MRP II.* John Wiley & Sons, Inc.

About Oliver Wight and the Authors

Rod Hozack

Rod Hozack

With 15 years in the pharmaceutical industry and 20 years consulting, Rod has a wealth of hands-on experience. With a marketing background, where a depth of knowledge in demand management and forecasting is essential, Rod's expertise also covers strategy development and deployment, product development, production planning and execution, and Integrated Business Planning.

AT OLIVER WIGHT

Rod has delivered many successful business improvement programs with large blue-chip organizations, including Abbott Laboratories, British American Tobacco, Caterpillar, Fonterra, and George Weston Foods. He has also a well-developed expertise in global and multisite business-excellence transformations. An accomplished strategist, Rod has a proven record of effective implementations that deliver tremendous value for his clients.

Driven by an intense desire to bring the best out in people, Rod's focus is on coaching the executive to lead sustainable organizational change. He uses Oliver Wight's principles of Integrated Business Planning and Supply Chain Optimization and helps organizations implement the necessary supporting processes to achieve their strategic aspirations.

Rod pioneered the development of Oliver Wight's Integrated Tactical Planning methodology that enables organizations to establish robust processes and behaviors for managing short-term planning and execution in the most effective way.

INDUSTRY BACKGROUND

Starting his career as a professional athlete, Rod brings with him, and has applied, the principles of high performance to a wide range of industries, from traditional manufacturing, distribution, and marketing to FMCG companies and, more recently, medical services. Using his broad knowledge and experience, Rod set up a medical practice to demonstrate that best-practice disciplines for a physical-goods environment apply equally well in service businesses.

Prior to his move into consulting in 1999, Rod worked for a global pharmaceutical company, Pfizer, in a dual role, reporting to the President of Operations Asia Pacific, and the Vice President of Global Strategic Marketing. Here, he managed the value chain for a group of brands in Asia Pacific.

In his early career, Rod held several sales and marketing positions and led the set up, then management of, a division of Wyeth Australasia and Wyeth-Ayerst, for women's health, based in Australia.

He has an undergraduate degree in exercise physiology and a postgraduate degree in business, both of which required final-year, original-work theses. He continues to be a voracious learner and athlete and is always striving to apply the latest business excellence thinking in everything he does.

QUOTE

Designing and deploying global and multisite transformations, and watching people learn and develop along the way, is what I love doing. The key to successful transformations is engaging the leadership team and creating the right culture to drive success.

Stuart Harman

Stuart combines his extensive experience in operations, sales, supply chain, and general management gained in over 20 years working in manufacturing organizations around the world with his 12 years of experience at Oliver Wight, where he educates, coaches, and guides organizations so that their people can sustainably transform and improve their business and personal performance.

Stuart Harman

AT OLIVER WIGHT

A specialist in Integrated Business Planning, supply chain and process improvement, strategy execution, and Integrated Tactical Planning, Stuart has delivered transformation programs for organizations across multiple industries around the world including ANSTO, BAT, Chep, Cochlear, Dupont, Kimberly-Clark, Mondelez, Qantas, and Smorgon Steel. A skilled people manager and an analytical and innovative change agent, Stuart works in partnership with his clients to realize significant, sustainable benefits across their businesses

INDUSTRY BACKGROUND

Prior to joining Oliver Wight, Stuart gained extensive experience within the fast-moving consumer goods (FMCG) environment, working on improvement projects and all facets of operations, in particular supply chain management. Stuart held numerous roles at Australian Pet Brands (formerly Bush's Pet Foods), the leading manufacturer of private label and branded pet foods. Working with the multisite manufacturer engaged in contract manufacture, Stuart helped with the development of both their own brands and private label products for the leading supermarket chains across the Asia Pacific region. As a supply chain manager, Stuart was responsible for the planning, purchasing, warehouse, distribution, and customer service across the multisite operation. He successfully reduced inventories by 55% ($10 million reduction in working capital) through improved planning, purchasing, and inventory management practices. Through his time with the Luxfer Group, Stuart worked on two successful Oliver Wight Class A implementation programs in the UK and Australia. He also developed and led a number of business and quality-improvement programs in Luxfer's European and Asia Pacific businesses. A confident and passionate communicator with excellent presentation skills, Stuart has a bachelor of engineering (honors) degree in engineering with industrial management and a master's degree in business administration.

QUOTE

Business improvement relies on the integration of people and behavior with new processes and tools. Failure to sufficiently invest in people will fatally undermine the success of any change program.

Todd Ferguson

Todd Ferguson

With more than two decades of experience in sales, order fulfillment, and demand management, Todd brings insights and solutions to help companies achieve improved and sustained financial performance.

AT OLIVER WIGHT

Todd has successfully helped companies realize tangible improvements in demand management, Integrated Business Planning, and Integrated Tactical Planning. He has helped lead account teams as well as coached clients across a wide range of companies and industries, including Facebook, General Electric, Kraft Foods, and Tiffany. Todd is the lead instructor of the Oliver Wight America's Demand Management Education course.

INDUSTRY BACKGROUND

Prior to joining Oliver Wight, Todd worked as the demand manager at Weir Oil & Gas, an upstream oil and gas leader that specializes in the manufacture of high-pressure well service pumps and related flow control equipment. In that role, he drew on his skill as a demand planning expert to help define and continuously improve the company's Integrated Business Planning process. At St. Jude Medical (now Abbott) he was directly involved in the design and implementation of planning solutions for this international medical device manufacturer and was asked to lead a cross-functional team in the development and implementation of a global S&OP process. Todd has written and coauthored white papers in subjects including demand control, demand segmentation, strategy, and Integrated Business Planning. He has conducted public and private courses about demand management, Integrated Business Planning, and Integrated Tactical Planning. Todd has also presented to industry conferences and graduate-level classes and has earned the APICS Certified Supply Chain Professional (CSCP) designation. Todd holds a BA (economics) from the University of British Columbia.

QUOTE

Change is inevitable and occurring at a faster pace than ever before. Successful organizations are constantly seeking methods to adapt and improve business outcomes. I am fortunate to have met and worked with individuals and teams who thrive on the challenge that change brings and who embrace improvement initiatives that solve real problems.

Dawn Howarth

DAWN HOWARTH

With more than 20 years of experience in global supply chain and ERP design across international markets, Dawn brings a pragmatic and practical approach to organizational development.

AT OLIVER WIGHT

At Oliver Wight, Dawn provides education and training to aid organizations implementing Integrated Business Planning and supply chain optimization processes. As a consultant, Dawn has built years of experience advising on transition services for acquisitions and divestments. Dawn believes effective communication based on a culture of trust is the key to the success of any organization, and education and teamwork are essential to achieving this goal.

INDUSTRY BACKGROUND

Prior to joining Oliver Wight, Dawn held the position of supply chain manager at Flexsys, a multinational organization specializing in chemical production. Dawn was responsible for planning five product groups across Europe and America and in designing and implementing the company's business processes.

During Dawn's decade-long career at Flexsys, she held a variety of roles including supply manager, demand manager, and global ERP manager. In these roles Dawn worked extensively in Europe, the Americas, and Asia, gaining insight into cultural sensitivities and different approaches to business.

In 2001 Dawn worked with Oliver Wight on the Flexsys Global Class A project, initially developing the revised MRP system for the whole organization before providing rollout support for both S&OP and execution processes across all worldwide locations. Dawn then moved on to process design, driven by a view that for S&OP to succeed the main functions of demand, supply, customer service, and purchasing had to be thought of as a whole.

Dawn is a certified Six Sigma Green Belt. She holds a degree in business administration from Wolverhampton University.

QUOTE

Inventory is not something to tackle simply when a major problem strikes. As supply chains become longer and more complex, and global economic volatility remains, taking control of inventory is essential to cost-effectively meet the demands of today's consumer. Inventory is a consequence.

Index

Page numbers followed by *f* refer to figures.

in materials requirement
planning, 121*f*
Time frames, and resource
planning, 58
Time horizons, setting, 22
Trading zone:
in make-to-order supply
environment, 104
in make-to-stock supply
environment, 102*f*
Training, in sustainability plan,
169–171

U

Universal Equation, 118, 119*f*

V

Value stream mapping, 142
Variables, defining, 37
Velocity improvements, 59
Velocity measures,
141–142, 142*f*
Velocity ratio, 142*f*

W

Weekly planning process, 156*f,*
158*f. See also* Daily-weekly
cadence
Weekly realignments, 6